Crea
Your O
Happiness

Also by Nancy Ashley

Create Your Own Reality: A Seth Workbook

Create Your Own Happiness

A Seth Workbook

Nancy Ashley

PRENTICE HALL PRESS

New York   London   Toronto   Sydney   Tokyo

The ideas and suggestions presented in this book, as they relate to your health, are not intended to substitute for proper medical advice.

The extracts on pages 102–106 are reprinted by permission of The Putnam Publishing Group from *To Love is to Be Happy With* by Barry Neil Kaufmann. Copyright © 1977 by Barry Neil Kaufmann.

Prentice Hall Press
Gulf + Western Building
One Gulf + Western Plaza
New York, New York   10023

PRENTICE HALL PRESS and colophon are registered trademarks of Simon & Schuster, Inc.

Library of Congress Cataloging in Publication Data

Ashley, Nancy.
  Create your own happiness: a Seth workbook/Nancy Ashley.—1st ed.
    p.   cm.
  ISBN 0-13-189226-6
  1. Spirit writings.   2. Happiness.   I. Title.   II. Title: Seth workbook.
BF1301.A72 1988
133.9'3—dc19   88–3115

Manufactured in the United States of America

10 9 8 7 6 5 4 3 2 1

First Edition

Contents

Preface

For two months during the summer of 1984 I had a house guest who came from California to stay at my seaside cottage on Oahu's north shore and to work with me, using my soon-to-be published Seth workbook *Create Your Own Reality* as a focus. Every day we'd spend hours talking, sitting on the screened porch, each of us with a cat or two in our laps, looking out at the sparkling sea and crashing waves, as the cool trade winds swept around us.

Magna saw me as her mentor, but I didn't see her as my student, for certainly I learned as much from her as she did from me. She asked me many deep and challenging questions that tested to the limits my understanding of the Seth material and led to insights I wished I'd incorporated in my book. This woman had been intensely unhappy for most of her life (despite her intelligence, beauty, and talent) and was determined to change. We had met on the mainland a few months earlier and had felt an instant empathy with each other. When Magna began reading the manuscript of my book, she recognized that she was on to something—much as I had recognized in first reading the Seth material some ten years before that I was on to something. She then asked if she could study with me in the summer. I didn't have a new writing project going at the time and was glad to have her. It felt as if I'd shot my wad with *Create Your Own Reality,* for it had been a great challenge to distill from the complex and voluminous Seth material what I considered to be the most important concepts, to explain them clearly, and then to devise exercises that would implement those concepts. At the same time, I wanted very much to do more writing about the Seth philosophy, which I was continuing to find so valuable in my everyday personal life.

Each morning Magna wrote in her journal for a couple of hours; she did an exercise from one of the chapters of the book and described her reaction to it. Then we'd sit on the porch and talk. She was intellectually stimulated by the concepts and found the exercises useful in unearthing beliefs she had not been aware of. Like so many people I'd talked to about the Seth material, she found it difficult at first to accept its most basic principle: We totally create our own reality through the beliefs we hold. Like so many others before her in talking about some unfortunate past event, she would ask, "But why would I create a reality like that for myself?" Soon, though, after she began to discover some of the beliefs that she had about herself, she could see why.

Magna could see that her reality was in keeping with the beliefs that she held. Basically those beliefs were that she was unworthy, helpless, and unattractive. She had "bought" these beliefs when growing up, and they were still operating even though she was now in her mid-thirties. Interestingly enough, Magna knew intellectually that none of these beliefs about her was "true," but she still believed them. Her "rational" mind told her that it was nonsense to believe such things about herself, but her emotions (which are *always* generated by beliefs) told her otherwise.

Even so, there was a lot of comfort for Magna (as there had been for me and others I'd known) in really coming to see that her own beliefs had created her space-time experiences. Her beliefs were "unrealistic," but at least they explained why she had gone through what she had. Before that revelation, she had not understood at all why she had failed so utterly to find happiness. All her life it had seemed to her that she was unlucky, that fate did not smile on her as it did, so inexplicably, on others. In coming to see that she had created what she had for herself through her beliefs, Magna gained a sense of control over her destiny that she had not felt before. She was not at the mercy of fate, only at the mercy of her beliefs.

So then Magna was ready for the next step—to get rid of those beliefs she didn't like, which had created a reality of unhappiness, and to replace them with beliefs that would create a happier reality for herself. And it was at this stage that she balked. I was not surprised, for other people I'd worked with had, over time, come to accept the idea that they were responsible for creating their own reality and that their beliefs determined what that reality would be. They really came to see this clearly. But when it came to getting rid of any of their beliefs, they resisted. For a while this puzzled me until I finally came to see that, for the most part, people tend to regard their beliefs as an essential part of their identity: Their beliefs are who they are; they *are* their beliefs. In other words, they can't get rid of their beliefs without getting rid of themselves. Self-annihilation!

I had tried to get these people to see beliefs in a different light by using Seth's analogy, which compares beliefs to furniture that can be rearranged or thrown out at will. But this didn't seem to help in most cases, perhaps because furniture is so obviously physical and beliefs are so obviously *not* physical (until their results appear in space-time reality). They still continued to see their beliefs as *themselves*. And so, like Magna, the people I'd worked with might accept intellectually the idea of changing beliefs, but emotionally they resisted it (because of their belief that they would annihilate themselves). And I didn't know what to do about this. It seemed to me another analogy was needed. As it turned out, Magna was the one to provide it.

One day we were discussing an exercise she had just done, and, as had happened many times before, she'd discovered some beliefs that she hadn't been aware of. But, as usual, instead of being glad that she had finally brought these beliefs to light, she got down on herself for having had them to begin with. As she had done many times before, Magna used the discoveries she had made in doing the exercise not as a means of changing herself but as yet another way of supporting the old beliefs she had about herself, "proving" that she was unworthy by having the beliefs. Exasperated, I pointed this out to her. Emotionally, she responded, "I just can't help it, Nancy. I'm *habituated* to unhappiness!"

We looked at each other and our faces simultaneously lit up. We both knew a breakthrough in understanding had occurred. We hadn't seen the situation in quite that light before. Of course, once we did see it, it seemed so obvious, as all truths do: What Magna thought about herself, that is, the beliefs she held that led to her feeling unhappy, were nothing more than habits. Habits of mind. She was habituated to unhappiness. How could it be, I thought to myself, that I had never before viewed beliefs in quite this manner—as habits?

The perspective was so useful because everyone *knows* what habits are. Everyone *has* habits. Furthermore, everyone knows that habits are not who they are: Habits are not *them,* but something they *do.* And finally everyone knows that habits can be changed with determined effort. Everyone has experienced habits and has experienced changing habits, so they know for sure that changing habits does not at all annihilate their personhood, although it does change their reality in some way. A perfect analogy! Especially since, unlike furniture, many habits are not physical at all, but mental, just as beliefs are mental. For instance, a friend once told me amusedly that when driving he was in the habit of mentally counting cars that were the same make as his own. He didn't know when he got into that habit, but now, every time he drove he mentally took note of each Colt he saw along the way. He even told me he had seen eight the day before, and that his record was fifty-six Colts spotted during an extended drive.

All of us have such "quirks"—mental habits we are aware of to varying degrees, which we may find amusing, as my friend did with his car-counting habit, or which we may find annoying. And if we find one that is annoying enough, we make an effort to stop doing it. I remember that a couple of years ago I realized I'd somehow got into the habit every weekday morning when I woke up of mentally going through the actions involved in getting myself out of the house and on the way to my teaching job at the university. "Get up. Brush teeth. Put on turquoise pants and lavender top. . . ." One day, I could see that I was boring myself with this mental routine and decided to stop doing it. The next morning I automatically started in on my internal recitation, caught myself doing it, and stopped. The next day the same thing happened. Within a week I had wiped out what had become an annoying, if harmless, mental habit.

Beliefs are a type of mental habit, a habitual way of thinking about the world. As mental habits, they are not who we are but rather something we do, mental actions we take, expressions we habitually choose. These habits of thought, then, like other mental or physical habits can be changed without affecting who we are while certainly affecting the reality we create for ourselves. For instance, once Magna had got past the hurdle of totally identifying with her beliefs, she made phenomenal progress in getting rid of those beliefs/habits that led to the creation of unhappiness for herself and replacing them with beliefs/habits that led to the creation of happiness. Her life has changed dramatically, and she is much happier now than she used to be. Still, she remains Magna. Rather than annihilating her selfhood through these changes, she has expanded, become *more* herself than she had ever dreamed she could be.

I hope this book will have the same effect on you. Or, rather, that in going through this book and doing the exercises and practicing the "Habits of Happiness" at the end of each chapter, you will create for yourself a happier, more expanded reality than you now have. It is up to you to do the work; this book cannot do it for you. But I hope it can inspire and motivate you to do the necessary work/play involved in self-searching and self-changing. To that end I have included a lot of personal examples from my life and the lives of people I've known, which I hope will show you that you are not alone. I think each person tends to feel he or she is the only one who has been through certain things, the only one who has reacted in such a way to a given situation. And, although it is true that each of us is unique, viewing the world from his or her own center, it is also true that we are all interconnected, united in our desire to learn and to grow and to see what our beliefs look like when dramatized in three-dimensional reality. We are all in this together, and the more aware we become of the beliefs under which others operate, the more aware we become of our own similar (or dissimilar) beliefs.

We create our own reality, whether we like it or not. I hope to make it clear that if you don't like some aspect of your reality, you can change it. Actually, you are always changing in any case, for that's what "life" is all about. But you can learn to have more conscious control over the changes you experience and the resulting realities created than you presently have. It is all a matter of bringing to conscious awareness those beliefs/habits of mind you have that result in realities you are not happy with and then replacing these beliefs/habits with others that create realities you *are* happy with. Earlier I gave you the example of the annoying mental habit I had of rehearsing every minute action before getting up in the morning. Like most habits, this one was invisible to me at first—I did not give it my conscious attention. And I would have had that habit to this day if I hadn't finally *attended to* it. What helped to draw my attention to it was an uncomfortable feeling, which I soon identified as boredom. I associated this discomfort with the mental habit, which gave me the motivation to stop doing it. But stopping took some practice, because it had become automatic for me to think that way in that situation—my habit wasn't a *conscious* process. I had to be on the alert for that automatic response, ready to notice it, so that I could then consciously stop it, nip it in the bud.

It is the same way with beliefs. You have to notice them before you can change them, and very often your feeling of discomfort will provide the first clue to the belief. Identifying the emotion (or, in other cases, the action, or the memory, or something else) will lead to identifying the belief. And once you see *that,* you are on your way. It is then a process of being alert to that belief/habit and of practicing with other potential beliefs/habits that you can see will create a more enjoyable reality for yourself. It is really quite a simple procedure, if not always *easy:* We are complex entities with many "parts" to ourselves and with many (sometimes conflicting) beliefs operating.

The more you can accept yourself as you are in each moment, the more open you will be to change—the more open you will be to accepting new beliefs about yourself that will expand your horizons. Conversely, the more you get down on yourself for having certain habits of mind (as Magna did at first), the more you will impede your progress—the more you will reject new beliefs about yourself that could change your life for the better. It may seem paradoxical, but self-acceptance is the key to change. You have to believe here and now that you're okay in order to believe that it is okay for you to have more, to be happy. That's why so many of the habits in this book are devoted to various forms of self-acceptance.

I genuinely wish you all success and happiness and evermore expansive realities. Have fun!

—Guerneville, California, 1988

Create
Your Own
Happiness

1

"It Is Not What Happens to Me . . ."

"It is not what happens to me, but my reactions or resistance that determine my 'feel good' or 'feel bad.' "

Many years ago I attended a workshop on self-esteem in which we were given a number of "affirmations" like the one above to memorize and repeat, the theory being that we would form new habits of thought in doing so and thus create a better life for ourselves.

This was the first time I'd heard such a notion: We could change the way we *thought* about things and thereby have a happier life. I wasn't at all sure this process of memorizing affirmations and saying them over and over again would do any good, but I was willing to give it a try, for if it *did* work the rewards for spending a few minutes every day on such an activity would be enormous.

And so, over the next few months I daily repeated selected affirmations from the book I'd been given at the workshop. I tried to sense the truth value, for me, of each statement—whether I not only believed it but believed I could put it into practice. Many of the statements did not seem relevant for me, and others seemed to be different ways of saying the same thing. But one affirmation, which soon became my favorite, continued to ring fresh and true after many repetitions. I liked it so much that I made a sign out of it and put it on the wall near my telephone, where I'd run into it regularly and where my friends would see it, too, for I hoped they'd find it as meaningful as I did. It went like this: "It is not what happens to me, but my reactions or resistance that determine my 'feel good' or 'feel bad.' "

At the time, the implication of this particular affirmation was, for me, profound: It meant I had a choice of how I responded in a situation, choosing to get upset about it or choosing to remain calm. This idea really appealed to me, for it meant that I was not at the mercy of fate, caught up in my feelings and out of control; I could *choose* how I reacted. Until that time it had never occurred to me that I had a choice about how I felt. I saw my emotions as automatic responses to events.

To use a mundane example (for it is around the most mundane events of our lives that we have formed the most habits), once a week I'd go to Safeway to do the week's shopping for my family of four. And every week I'd resist going—far from looking forward to this

1

event, I dreaded it. If you'd asked me why, I could have come up with several reasons: I resented having the responsibility of keeping food in the larder, of keeping track of what was needed and making sure I got it so that no one would complain. I might have said that the atmosphere of the store was unappealing with its canned music and chilly frozen-food sections and that I had many better things to do with my time than to spend it there. Whatever the reason, I always found myself uptight and in a hurry in the store and compulsive about getting everything on my list in the most efficient manner possible. If I passed an item by and had to go back to that aisle later, I'd be mad at myself for fouling up and at my family for laying the expectation on me to be the rememberer and the go-getter. By the time I got out of the store I would always be tired and irritable.

But after a couple of weeks of repeating "It is not what happens to me . . ." and thus keeping the idea in conscious awareness, I found that my weekly grocery shopping didn't feel as burdensome as it once had. When I sensed an oncoming dread at the thought of going shopping, I'd think, "I'm choosing to feel this and I can choose to feel differently." And just that realization, just making that statement to myself, was enough to change my mood to a more positive one. The idea that I had a choice in the matter was enough in itself to make me feel better. My negative reactions of before had been intensified by the belief that I had no choice, that I was stuck with my negative feelings.

Over a period of time my grocery shopping experience became more pleasant to the point where, today, I genuinely enjoy it: the fresh fruits and vegetables beautifully displayed, the ever-changing bargains, the customers I see regularly and those who are new to me, the checkers with their friendly greetings. Today it is so pleasant that it's hard to imagine how I conjured up the dread I did about grocery shopping.

Seeing my feelings as chosen, not foisted upon me by other people and/or circumstances, was what it took to deal with recurring incidents in my life that "made" me unhappy—incidents I was in the habit of reacting to in a negative way out of a belief that I had no choice. Seeing the way I habitually reacted and then believing that I had a choice gave me a sense of power over my own life that I hadn't felt before. I often found that by saying to myself "I am choosing to be angry"—or sad, or disappointed—made the anger, or the sadness, or the disappointment seem much less negative than before because then those feelings did not have attached to them the belief that I was helplessly responding to what was forced upon me. I also found that saying to others "I have chosen to feel angry about this" rather than "You make me angry" kept communication going rather than breaking down, so that inevitably we found some way out of our difficulties with one another.

Later, as I looked back on the process I had gone through in forming this habit of happiness (the belief that I could choose my feelings), I saw that there were four phases to it. The first one was to *notice* that I was having a negative ("feel bad") reaction to a situation. Noticing one's response is easier to do in an unprecedented situation than it is in a recurring one, for in recurring situations we are in the *habit* of responding in a certain way—we do so automatically. Thus the situation and our response to it becomes inextricably related in our minds, so that just imagining the situation will elicit the associated feelings. For me, just thinking about going grocery shopping used to fill me with dread. I had to dissociate the feelings from the situation, to recognize that the situation itself was not inherently positive or negative but that my habitually chosen feelings made it seem that way. The negativity was not in the *situation* but in my *feelings* about it.

After noticing my negative responses, the next phase was for me to accept the idea that there were other ways to respond—that I had choices. This phase, of course, is the biggie, for it involves changing the belief—the habit of mind—that says there is no choice to one that says there is. The affirmation I had been repeating helped me make that change, for I came to *believe*—to really believe—what I was saying after so many repetitions.

But even if you believe you can choose your response, this does not necessarily mean you'll *want* to. It could be you're getting certain rewards from your anger, from your self-righteousness, from your feeling of helplessness. It may be that you are learning to deal with anger for the first time and to enjoy expressing it, it may be that you enjoy "making" others feel guilty, or it may be that you don't want to take on the responsibility inherent in making a conscious choice. In order to change your feelings/behavior, you not only need to notice them and to accept the belief that you have a choice but you also have to *want* to make a different choice. Only then will you take *action*.

Noticing, believing, wanting, and *acting* are the four phases of the process involved in creating the first habit of happiness in this book. To give you some practice in this process, the exercise that follows asks you, first, to denote your habitual responses in various everyday situations—those in which you may come away feeling bad much of the time—then to believe that you have a choice in your response, then to ask yourself whether you want to feel and act differently, examining the payoffs you may be getting from your response (perhaps there are more "feel goods" than "feel bads" in that situation after all!), and then to decide whether to make the same choice, all things considered, or to make a different choice the next time, envisioning some possible new responses and actions. Here goes.

Exercise

1. What is your habitual response to getting stuck in a rush-hour traffic jam? Do you believe you have a choice in how you respond? If not, why? What beliefs can you see associated with a belief in not having a choice? What are the consequences ("feel goods" and "feel bads") of that habitual response? If you do feel you have a choice, do you still choose to respond in the same way in the future? If so, acknowledge this choice every time it's made; this will weaken the "feel bads." If you do want to change your response, think of other preferable ways of responding to the situation and of the outcomes of these responses.

2. What is your habitual response to having to wait in a long line at the bank? Do you believe you have a choice in how you respond? What are the consequences of that response? Do you still choose to respond in the same way in the future? If not, think of other preferable ways of responding to the situation and envision the outcome.

3. What is your habitual response to having to fix a flat tire? Do you believe you have a choice in how you respond? What are the consequences of that response? Do you still choose to respond in the same way in the future? If not, think of other preferable ways of responding and envision the outcome.

4. What is your habitual response to having someone's anger directed at you? Do you believe you have a choice in how you respond? What are the consequences of that response? Do you still choose to respond in the same way in the future? If not, think of other preferable ways of responding and envision the outcome.

5. What is your habitual response to failure in accomplishing or attaining a goal? Do you believe you have a choice in how you respond? What are the consequences of that response? Do you still choose to respond in the same way in the future? If not, think of other preferable ways of responding and envision the outcome.

6. Think of a recurring situation in which your response does not feel good to you. Do you believe you have a choice in how you

respond? What are the consequences of that response? Do you choose to respond the same way the next time or to respond differently? If differently, what are other preferable ways of responding and what outcome do you envision?

Habit of Happiness #1

Notice your habitual "feel bad" responses to everyday situations. *Believe* you have a choice in your response. Ask yourself whether you *want* to make a different choice, considering all the consequences. If you do not want change, continually acknowledge that you are choosing that response. If you do want change, envision another response, and after considering its possible outcome, take *action*.

2

We Are All Playwrights

Five years after I attended the self-esteem workshop mentioned in chapter 1 and first discovered the technique of repeating ideas you want to believe until you believe them, I began reading the Seth material. Although Seth didn't call beliefs "habits of mind" in those days (he does in his later books), he did say that we tend to regard beliefs as facts: We are so used to viewing the world in a certain way—from believing certain things about it—that we don't recognize the beliefs as *only* beliefs but take them to be facts about life. This idea is closely related to the "beliefs as habits" one. For instance, if we habitually believe, say, that the world is a dangerous place, we will habitually create that reality for ourselves. Then we'll look "out there" at that reality and say, "See, it's a *fact* that the world is a dangerous place." So, our habits of mind seem like facts to us.

After reading just a little bit of *Seth Speaks* I came to realize that my favorite affirmation, "It is not what happens to me, but my reactions or resistance that determine my 'feel good' or 'feel bad,' " had a belief ("fact of life") underlying it that was so obvious I hadn't even thought about it. And yet this belief, this habit of mind, had limiting consequences. Although embracing the concept of "it is not what happens to me . . ." might be a good first step along the way to becoming more free and happy, I could see that by continuing to hold on to the idea now, after reading what Seth had to say, I would be limiting myself in creating the best possible reality for myself.

The basic assumption underlying the "it is not what happens to me . . ." affirmation is that there is a "real world" out there with which we come in contact and interact with—a world of events and happenings independent of us. Thus the only thing we can do is to make the best of whatever comes. We can choose to be upset or not upset with what the world brings us, but we cannot choose what is brought.

This may seem to be a small point. What difference does it make, you may ask, whether or not we choose the event so long as we choose our reactions to it? The main thing is to quit letting things upset us, right? Wrong. For to the extent that we *believe* events happen to us without our having any input into their production, to the extent that we *believe* something out there happens to us, we will be prevented from seeing how much power, how much influence we really do have. We will continue to see our world as something separate from ourselves, an objective reality (in the parlance of modern science) that we can only learn to make the best of but can never really have much influence on. To the extent that we *believe* all this we will not be in touch with our own importance and power in creating our own realities.

According to Seth, we are literally the creator of our world. Whatever happens to us, whatever events come into our lives, we have created. We not only have a choice as to how to react to the events in our lives but also have the choice as to which events occur in the first place. And if we don't like our realities, we can change them. It is not simply a matter of adjusting to what happens to us or of deciding to make the best of a situation—though, indeed, that is a good skill to learn—but a matter of changing our lives in such a way that we no longer feel things happening *to* us but know we're *making* them happen.

It's the difference between being in a play written and directed by someone else, in which the main lesson is how to do the best job we can with our assigned parts, or being the writer, director, and all the actors in an ever-changing play. In the first situation we can get some sense of power in being on stage and handling our roles with inspiration and insight, but think of how much more powerful we are going to feel if we can change the lines, the plot, the setting, and the characters in the play at will. Yet, according to Seth that quite literally is what we can do, and what in fact we *are* doing all the time, whether or not we are aware of it. Creating our own realities—creating habits of happiness, if you will—is not so much a matter of learning to do something we haven't previously learned how to do as it is a matter of bringing to conscious awareness the process we go through all the time. And before we can do that we have to give up the belief that the world happens *to* us, that we can't control the events in our lives, that accidents, poor health, the loss of a job, the failure of a romance are events done to us rather than events we create.

Of course, the reason most of us believe in the world "out there" happening to us is that just about everyone else does! This is a basic mass belief—a taken-for-granted fact of life—that we have never questioned. (We will discuss mass beliefs in chapter 6.) It may seem to you even now as you read this that "the objective world out there" is an unquestionable concept reflecting the true state of affairs.

But if you can for a moment suspend your belief in the truth of "the objective world" and agree to imagine it being some other way, you will be rewarded by many clues from the past pointing to the reality of each of us as a playwright/director/actor. I am sure all of you can think of little "dramas" in your life when you had a definite feeling of having brought events about through your own attitude and/or actions. Suspend your belief for a moment in the idea that events happen *to* us and concentrate on the idea the we first "write" the plays that we will later star in (in our imaginations, in our dreams); that we then select the cast of characters who will play different roles in relation to us (these characters, "in the wings" beforehand, agree to be in our dramas for what they can learn from them—just as we agree to play in their dramas); and that we then act in the plays, seeing how our beliefs look "out there" in three-dimensional reality. If you can for the moment focus on this idea, you will then begin to remember times in your life when you did indeed feel that you were in a play that you had already written.

I vividly recall an episode in my life when I felt as if I were acting in *two* plays going on simultaneously. It wasn't until the dramas were drawing to a close that I understood why I had "written" them. This is often the case, for we set up these plays in order to learn from them; we don't know what we are learning until we've learned it! In this case, I was ready to give up a belief in my "fierce" independence (as myself and others described it) and to embrace interdependence and cooperation.

For years, my belief in self-sufficiency and independence had stood me in good stead. Before that I had struggled with a belief in my dependence (especially dependence on men), fearing that I was helpless on my own. To find out (come to believe) that I could be responsible for myself on many levels was very gratifying. However, as long as I held on to a belief in my fierce independence I limited myself to "going it alone." A cooperative, interdependent relationship with others—either in work or in love—was obviated by this belief.

So I created a reality—wrote a play for myself—involving three other "characters." The script called for myself and a man I'd recently met to be mates and nest-builders. The other two actors were his son and daughter-in-law. Their role (as carpenters in "real life") was to remodel the house I'd bought in exchange for part of the acreage where the old fixer-upper was located. The play opened with a lot of enthusiasm and goodwill. It seemed that everyone was happy with the arrangement. Soon, though, a rift occurred. One of the actors—my mate—played a competitive role rather than the cooperative one I thought had been agreed upon. Responding angrily to any situation in which he didn't get to have everything his way, he claimed at the same time that I was getting all the attention and he was getting none, that he got no consideration and I got it all, that my ideas were valued and his weren't. And he felt it was up to *me* to change this.

In the meantime, the other three players continued in a cooperative mode, doing the best we could to show the fourth that we did not see the situation in the same light at all: We saw him as having his own way a lot, as getting a lot of attention, consideration, and respect. But it seemed that he wanted it *all*.

Well, the house got fixed up but the matehood failed. And the lesson for me was that cooperation and interdependence work, but competition does not. In this case, the competition was between dependence and independence. I didn't see this, as I said, until close to the end. This man *depended* on us—me, especially—for a feeling of self-worth. He did not, himself, believe he was worthy and expected us to give him that belief. Up against this heavy dependency came my fierce independence. The more determined the man was to get strokes from me, the less I was willing to give them. There was no way for the two of us to get together; we were at opposite poles.

By having both plays going on at once I could contrast my old belief in the value of independence with my emerging belief in the value of interdependence. I came to see clearly that a belief in independence inevitably leads to conflict while a belief in interdependence leads to harmony where polarities do not exist, where giving and receiving are different aspects of the same thing.

Exercise

1. Look back to some dramatic times in your life. You may have consciously realized you were playing different roles with different people; you may have recognized that great changes were happening; you may have been aware that your emotions were particularly strong, that the outcomes were climactic—or all of these elements. List all of the dramas in your life you can think of.
2. Choose one of these dramas. Why did you choose this one over the others?
3. What beliefs did you decide to dramatize as the writer of this play?
4. What lessons did you seek to teach/learn through this dramatization?
5. Why did you select the particular characters and give them their particular roles?
6. Why do you think the other "actors" agreed to be in the play? What lessons were they hoping to learn? Do you think these were the same lessons you learned, or different ones?
7. How do the settings and the props in the play reflect the beliefs of the characters?
8. Do you like the outcome of the play? What are other possible outcomes?
9. Have you written other plays with different outcomes as a result of having written this play first?

Habit of Happiness #2

Think of yourself as the playwright of your continuing life drama. Look upon everyone you meet as a character in the play you have written. Try to understand what beliefs are being dramatized and what each person's role is in the drama. Look for the lessons to be learned. Look on your environment and your possessions as being there for a purpose—to symbolize in three-dimensional reality various beliefs you hold. Realize that if you don't like the play you can change it.

3

Patting Ourselves
on the Back

I think there are two main reasons why people find the concept that
we literally create our own reality a truly difficult one to accept. One
reason is that we can't conceive of how this process would work:
What dynamics would be behind such a process? How does the play
written in our imagination or dreams become a space-time reality? I'll
have more to say about this later. The other reason is that we cannot
understand *why* we would choose the reality that we have, or certain
aspects of it: Interestingly enough, we are all usually quite willing to
pat ourselves on the back when it comes to the positive areas in our
lives. Success in business, a good marriage, a talent we've developed
make us feel proud. It wasn't someone "out there" who did it for us
or to us (though we may acknowledge good luck or timely advice):
We did it for ourselves. When it comes to what's good about our reality, we can usually see that it was of our own making.

That is, when we *notice* the good. Much of the time we concentrate on the bad—what isn't working in our lives, all of the negative
happenings. We do this not only because the negatives cause us discomfort but also because they *stand out* because they are unusual.

The truth is, there are many, many more "goods" in our lives than
"bads." We would not be able to survive if this were not the case, if
it were not for the marvelous cooperation inherent on all levels of our
being—from cells to organs to families to nations. We each exist as an
integral part of a vast interconnected network, which functions as a
unified whole—an ecosystem—in which every part contributes to and
is inextricable from the whole. Harmony is the sine qua non of our
being—the essence out of which we form our experience. This essence
(call it harmony, cooperation, love, or whatever) is reflected back at
us through our creations: our bodies, our actions, the natural environment, even man-made items. We take this harmony very much for
granted; it is a given. So, the only time we tend to notice the harmonious occurrences in our lives is when they are unprecedented or when
they are pleasantly anticipated events, such as winning a race or publishing a book. But the everyday harmonies of life—our hearts steadily
beating away, dandelions flashing yellow in a field, bees humming la-
zily on a summer morning—go unnoticed.

Instead, we concern ourselves with the few unharmonious ("bad"

14

feeling) aspects of our lives. These make us uncomfortable precisely because they are unusual—not in keeping with the harmony of our beings. And to some extent, this focus is as it should be, for it is around disharmony that we have lessons to learn and to grow from. Essentially, we all seek to be in harmony at all times. It is our natural way of being, and so we work to bring those areas of disharmony in our lives into harmony. This is what growth is all about—increasing our sense of harmony.

However, we tend to focus too much on what isn't right in our lives to the point where we believe life is mostly negative. This belief in turn leads to the creation of yet more negatives, and soon we are faced with the "fact" that life is negative. And if we really do believe that we create our own reality, we may then get down on ourselves for having done this to ourselves. So it is important to have the perspective that most of what we create is good and harmonious, and to pat ourselves on the back for these creations. When noticing something negative about ourselves or the world, it is an especially good practice then to look at something positive that is related to it.

For instance, say you have a cold. Your nose is stuffed up, your throat is sore, and your energy seems low. You notice this because it is not the usual harmonious state of affairs with your body. At this time, make it a point also to acknowledge those ways in which your body *is* in harmony: your steadily beating heart, your growing fingernails, your fine straight teeth. No detail is too minute to take notice of and to feel good about.

Some people have difficulty complimenting themselves. They are so into the habit of mind of observing all of the unharmonious aspects of their lives—and telling themselves how they have fouled up—that they have come to believe there's nothing good about themselves. And yet, because they crave to believe otherwise, they look "out there" for the support they cannot give themselves. They may hope, through complimenting others, to get compliments themselves. Or they may put themselves down before others, hoping that the others will disagree and tell them they're okay. But even if they do get compliments by these means, these people don't believe what others tell them because they don't believe in their own inherent goodness. They're insatiable; no amount of positive feedback from others can change their belief in their "no good" self. But they keep trying.

In chapter 1 I talked about the technique of repeating an affirmation until it becomes a part of your belief system and about how your reality changes because of this new habit of mind. The same principle applies here. By repeatedly complimenting yourself on whatever good you can come up with, you will come to believe in your own goodness, or strengthen your already existing belief. And your reality will change to reflect this heightened goodness back to you.

I had a lot of fun writing out "self-back-patting exercises," as I called them. Every day for about six months it was a part of my daily routine to sit down at the typewriter and write to myself about all the good things I had created and to compliment myself for them. It was always exhilarating to see how many unnoticed, taken-for-granted aspects of myself and my world I could come up with. Getting the long list down on paper where I could look at it worked better than merely sitting and thinking about it. For me, it was as if the physical act of writing down my thoughts gave more power to them, assuring their recurrence in the future. Some of you may find that visualizing the good things about yourself or what you have done will give you the same feeling that writing out my compliments gave me. But in any case, here is a short excerpt from my journal that focuses on the good things about different parts of my body.

Hands, you are so wonderful! Look at all the things you do for me. Why, I wouldn't be typing this without you. And look at the way your fingers fly over the keys so speedily. You make the writing task so very much more easy for me, you are indispensable to it. And typing is just one of the many, many things you do every day for me. From morning til night you are busy—dressing me, brushing my hair, cooking breakfast, gathering wood and chopping it, making a fire. And you hold the broom and the dustpan when I clean. You dial the phone for me, and you hang it up when the conversation is over. You do so many things that I have taken for granted until just now that I am truly astonished. Why without you I couldn't open a door or drive a car or zip up my jacket or wave to a friend or turn the pages in a book. Oh, hands, you are so good to me! And—I almost forgot—without you I could not pat myself on the back for having created you, who do all of these good things for me.

The following exercise gives you some areas of "goods" to explore.

Exercise

1. What are some good things your *hands* can do? Your *feet?* Your *tongue?*
2. What are some good things you *own?*
3. What are some good things you have *learned?*
4. What are your *skills?*
5. Who are some good *friends* to you?
6. What are some things you enjoy *eating?*
7. What are some things you enjoy *watching?*
8. What are some good things that have *happened* to you?
9. What are some good things you've *done?*
10. What are some good things in your *living environment?*
11. What are some things in the *natural environment* that you appreciate?
12. What are you *proud* of?
13. What makes you *happy?*

Habit of Happiness #3

Notice and pat yourself on the back for the many good things in your life—you created them! Especially when you are having a negative thought about yourself, think of something positive you have created in the same area and be proud of yourself for that.

4

How Our Beliefs Become Our Reality

In chapter 3 I said that when it comes to the good things that happen to us we are usually quite willing to accept the responsibility for having created those realities, if we notice them at all. But what about the negative things in life? What about, for instance, getting a speeding ticket? Why would we choose to have *that* happen to us? True, it's not the end of the world, but it's certainly an inconvenience, and what's the point of it all anyway? And what about the truly devastating happenings in our lives, such as serious illness, meeting with violence, getting laid off from a job, or finding out our best friend betrayed us? Now it is true, we'll admit, that *sometimes* an unhappy event may have been brought about by us, by some mistaken action or failure on our part. But a lot of the time—most of the time it seems—we can't see that there is *anything* we did to bring the event on. It happened *to* us despite what we wanted to happen and we had no control over it. And anyway, we didn't *want* these things to happen, so why would we *choose* to have them happen?

I have a beautiful friend, a small blond woman with three school-age children and a loving husband. One sunny morning after her husband had gone to work and her children to school, she was ambushed in her bedroom by a powerful dark man with a knife and raped. Why would she create such a reality for herself? Why, even to suggest such a thing is heresy! No one would *choose* to create such a reality for oneself. No, it may be that we have some choice in what our reality is or in how we react to the situation we're in, but to say that we create everything that happens to us, that we create this world—with its crime, violence, pollution, starvation, nuclear proliferation, racism, teenage suicide, alcoholism, drug addiction, child molesting, wife beating, poverty, misery, and disease—well, that's just too much to swallow!

Although it may seem difficult to accept responsibility for those aspects of our reality that we dislike, there is, at the same time, a great advantage to doing so: If we admit we are doing it to ourselves, we can do something about it. And if we believe we can do something about it, *that* will become our reality. Whatever we believe in, we will create for ourselves. As far as I'm concerned, to be strictly pragmatic, the best reason to accept the belief that we create our own reality is that this belief puts us in control of our own destiny. Once we admit our destiny is of our own creation, we empower ourselves to create the best possible destiny for ourselves and those around us.

Let's say, then, we do decide to accept the premise that we create our own reality. The question of *why* we create what we do still remains. Why would we choose to get a speeding ticket? Why would we choose to lose a job, get divorced, get cancer, or be raped?

The answer, according to Seth, is that we have certain beliefs about the world, about other people and ourselves, that govern the choices we make. Each of us is like an incredibly complex radio station that is constantly sending out messages and receiving them. Instead of sending and receiving radio waves, though, we exchange energy—conscious energy. In fact, energy and consciousness are two ways of looking at the same thing. Energy is consciousness in motion. Consciousness is made manifest by energy.

Imagine yourself as a radio station continually sending out conscious energy, that is, thoughts, and receiving thoughts. Some of those thoughts are in words but most of them are images. I don't think it is too difficult to imagine, for I am sure each of you has had the experience of suddenly becoming aware of your thoughts, of the images in your head. You seem to step aside in your mind and look at your thoughts as separate entities instead of integral parts of yourself. "Hmm, look at *that* idea I'm having, and *that* one. How interesting." People who meditate often report that they observe their thoughts in this detached manner. I once had the experience of seeing my thoughts clicking before me like images in a slot machine, although much faster and more varied, but somehow related to each other in a way I felt but could not express. What a kaleidoscope of juxtaposed ideas, each one leading to the next and also reminiscent of what came before! It was a remarkable experience.

Whenever energy exists, then, consciousness, that is, thoughts, exist. And since we are surrounded at all times by an aura of energy (as Kirlian photography has shown), we are also surrounded by thoughts—an aura of thought-filled energy. Now, at this point I want to make a distinction between thoughts and beliefs. Every thought has the potential of being a belief to any given person. But we do not believe everything we think—thank God! We see many thoughts come and go that we don't believe and that therefore do not affect our reality in any way. Other people may see the same thoughts, take them on as beliefs, and thus affect their reality. What makes a thought or image a belief is its *significance* to the individual. Depending on our past experience, our dreams, our imagination, and our higher purposes, we have constructed patterns of thought, or belief systems, which help us make sense of all the data coming in and guide us in our decision making and, thus, the reality we create. We are constantly sifting through the data coming in, looking for those of significance to us, those that fit into our already established patterns, that is, those we *expect* to manifest. This expectation adds an intensity to the thought, charging it with extra energy. This extra charge of energy is what makes manifestation possible; it enables us to form a material counterpart from our inner experience, so that we can experience the thought in physical reality. Beliefs, then, are expectant thoughts—thoughts charged with expectations. Perhaps it's more meaningful to call them pregnant ideas!

So again, picture yourself as a radio station surrounded by this cloud of thoughts, this aura of potential beliefs, and, like a magnet, attracting to it and impregnating those ideas that are compatible with it and repelling those that aren't. Some radio stations (other people with highly charged beliefs of a similar nature) will be drawn to your broadcast and you to theirs, while other stations' (people's) broadcasts will be static-filled or so weak you can hardly hear them. Your antennae will be up, endlessly scanning the "skies," monitoring the multitude of thoughts dashing about, on the lookout for those to zero in on. Like a magnet, you'll attract to you those that fit into your system (your expectations/beliefs), and you'll very adroitly keep those that don't at a distance. You will then use this energy you've attracted to you to create your space-time reality. You will find all sorts of clever ways to symbolize your beliefs in space-time, for you are nothing if not creative—constantly refining and revising, trying out new ways, discarding some and emphasizing others, using the feedback you get from experiencing your beliefs in material reality.

You will decide to discard some beliefs after a while because they no longer serve the purpose they once did. I'm thinking, for instance, of the belief Seth mentioned in not trusting anyone over thirty. That belief may have served you well in your twenties, getting you to take responsibility for yourself rather than depending on parents or mentors. But if you want to continue being responsible and trusting yourself, you'll have to give up that belief after you're thirty, of course—if you're aware of it. Other beliefs you will not discard but rather adjust them to meet new challenges. And so on. All of this time you are learning to use consciousness creatively and to see what your inner experience looks like in the three-dimensional world. What we see "out there" is our inner experience in material form—solidified beliefs.

Being physical entities on this plane, with space and time so stretched out, is indeed a challenge, and sometimes we lose sight of the forest amid the trees, getting so caught up in the drama we are starring in that we forget we are also the playwright. We lose sight of the premises we have based our play on, of the beliefs we had decided to try out, and we start to feel that everything has gotten out of hand, that we no longer have control. Instead of having a lighthearted attitude toward beliefs, we take them very seriously, as unmitigated and unalterable facts rather than as a few of the infinite number of possibilities (thoughts) available to us in creating our reality. In short, we lose sight of our role as creator and lose sight of the beliefs/expectations we used in creating our reality. And because our beliefs are hidden from us, we do not know why our reality is the way it is, or how to change it.

Now let's go back to the story of my blond friend who was raped. I had met her two years before the incident, and during that time she had become more and more depressed. She seemed to have everything going for her—youth, beauty, wealth, a devoted family—and yet she felt increasingly unfulfilled and *powerless* to do anything about it. She had married right out of high school and did not believe she had the education or the skills necessary to find satisfying work. She read widely, casting about for a solution to her dilemma, but the more she read, the more she believed herself to be helpless. Her husband, a very busy man, was sympathetic but not really "there" for her when she verbally tried to work through her morass of feelings. And in any case, she saw him as part of the problem: A dynamic businessman, he was considerably older than she was. She compared herself to him and found herself even more lacking.

A few months before the rape, she had become addicted to cocaine. The only time she could feel good about herself was when she was high, but she had to take more and more of the drug to keep that feeling. She didn't like herself for this, and her addiction only increased her feeling of helplessness, of being a victim, at the mercy of the world "out there."

From this perspective and by using the radio station analogy, it is not difficult to see why my friend created the reality of rape for herself. Her beliefs and the fears generated by them were a perfect fit with those of a man who also believed himself to be basically powerless, who believed himself to be the victim of society, who believed that through victimizing someone physically weaker, he could "prove" to himself that he wasn't utterly helpless—for a while.

Had my friend been aware of her beliefs she could have worked to change them, but they were invisible to her. She saw herself as a victim of circumstances, unable to help herself. It took a drastic event like rape finally to get her in touch with what a belief in helplessness could lead to. The rape proved to be a turning point in her life, and shortly afterward she and her family moved back East. I have now lost touch with her, but I last heard my friend was working part time at a center for battered women, using the insights she had gained from her own experience to help others—and thereby to help herself.

In chapter 2 the purpose was to get us in touch with ourselves as the creators of our reality by seeing the events of our lives as self-written plays. From this detached perspective of playwright it is easier for us to see the beliefs we are trying out, to see the habits of mind which, from the perspective of actor in the play, seem to be facts about reality. This chapter has the same purpose: to get us in touch with our creator selves. But this time we will use the radio station analogy instead of the playwright analogy.

Exercise

1. Recall a time when you felt strongly attracted to, or that you attracted, something—a person, an ideal, an action. Imagine yourself as a radio station with your antennae up, monitoring all of the conscious energy surrounding you. As vividly as possible, imagine your radio station–self drawing to you the thought of that person, ideal, or action. See your expectation (the belief that the thought will manifest) give an additional charge to the energy of that thought, and impregnate it. See the pregnant thought come into your physical reality. Can you feel the magnetic power—the extra charge of energy—of that expectation/belief?

2. Now think of any statement you don't believe at all, which is not a part of your reality (e.g., the goblins will get you; I am healthy/unhealthy, fat/skinny, etc.). Imagine yourself again as the radio station and see that thought go by your antennae, unattracted and unattractive. Can you *feel* the difference between a thought and a belief, between some thoughts you might have about reality and what you really do expect to happen?

Habit of Happiness #4

Notice the thoughts that *attract* you, and when you do, imagine the radio station analogy and see yourself impregnating those thoughts and making them a part of your reality. Remember, if you don't like what you are creating, you can always change your expectations and attract/impregnate ideas you prefer.

5

The Difference Between Beliefs and Ideals

As you read chapter 4 perhaps some of you said to yourselves, "What's all this about beliefs being hidden? I know what my beliefs are. I believe in God. I believe in truth. I believe in myself. I believe in equality. . . ."

Usually, statements like these are not about beliefs but about *ideals:* They are goals to reach for, values we seek to fulfill, rather than notions about reality. As Seth says, we are all idealists, born with an impetus toward "value fulfillment." We—including animals and plants and even minerals—are born with the idea that we are special, that no other entity sees the world quite as we do. And this is true: We have our unique perspectives, our own particular points of view, so that, even when we cooperate with many others in creating an epic drama in which to see our beliefs displayed en masse (and we'll have more to say about this in chapter 6), each of us sees the "same" drama from a more or less different perspective. Among us, we see every possible nuance in a situation, experiencing it from our own centers of being, which are like no others'. Through this we contribute to the overall understanding and growth of All That Is. This is value fulfillment.

This inborn impetus toward value fulfillment—an impetus toward the enrichment of our experience through understanding and growth—is not simply a selfish desire to improve our own lives in whatever way we can, then, but a desire to contribute to the improvement of all other life. What leads us always toward the best possible value fulfillment for ourselves automatically leads to the fulfillment of life in general.

So, although having ideals is necessary and good, at the same time it can cause us trouble here on earth when we inevitably fail to meet our goals and thus get down on ourselves or feel guilty—or when we blame *others* for failing to meet the ideals we have (consciously or unconsciously) set up for ourselves.

Many of the "shoulds" and "ought tos" of our daily lives are based on value fulfillment, on an idealized version of ourselves and what that entity would do. To use, once again, a mundane example, perhaps you say to yourself each morning, "I should have done the dishes last night!" Yet on the night before, when confronted with a sink of dirty dishes, you chose to watch TV instead of doing them. Now today here they are, still dirty. You get down on yourself for being lazy, or you get down on a family member for not doing them.

Now, why *should* you (or anyone) have done the dishes the night before? Might it be because you *believe* an efficient, organized, together person would have done them? And by not doing them you are demonstrating that you (or another family member) are not efficient, organized, and together? Efficiency, organization, and togetherness are ideals you have for yourself, goals you are working on in order to enhance your own life (and thereby all other life).

But if you really believed that you yourself (not just your idealized self) were efficient, organized, and together, you *would* be—you would create that reality for yourself. Whatever you believe, you will create for yourself. And, in fact, through believing you are not efficient, organized, and together, you are creating that reality instead.

As you can see, beliefs and values are closely intertwined. You have certain values, for yourself and for life in general, that you are seeking to fulfill. And you believe that a "good" person would perform in accordance with those values. You have the habit of mind that says it is "good" to do this and "bad" to do that. So, it is not the values per se that cause you difficulty, but your beliefs—habits of mind—that you are being good or bad through meeting or not meeting them.

For this reason, there's no need to get rid of these (seemingly at times unobtainable) ideals. They are necessary and good. Instead, it is necessary to get rid of those habits of mind surrounding your values, which get in the way of progress. If you believe that you are bad every time you do not live up to an ideal, this belief will hinder your progress in achieving that ideal. You will focus on your failures rather than your successes and thus create the reality of failure again and again. On the other hand, if you believe that you are always growing closer to your ideal, and that each failure is a lesson for you, a reminder, a gentle nudge in the right direction, then that will be your reality—growth rather than stagnation.

It is important to realize that people not only have different values but that they also often have different "shoulds" for the same values. Not doing the dishes right after eating may be perfectly okay for another person although it isn't for you. Perhaps that person does not value efficiency, organization, and togetherness, or perhaps his or her idea of being efficient, organized, and together means doing the dishes once a week, after all the dishes in the house have been dirtied. (Or, that particular person may not have any "shoulds"—though that is very unlikely.) However, this person doesn't think it's okay to drive to the supermarket a block away when one can walk, while you think it's perfectly okay to do that. He or she thinks it's inefficient to do so. You don't see it that way, though you value efficiency: You think driving there saves time. All kinds of everyday examples of this sort can cause trouble between people because of different ideals or because of different "shoulds" around the same ideals.

So, the very first step in forming a habit of happiness in this area is to let go of "shoulding" other people. Let them do this for themselves, if they must. Realize that the "shoulds" you have in mind are *your* "shoulds," and they are for *you* to deal with. Realize that, like you, other people are of good intent. Like you, they mean well. Like you, they have ideals they are seeking to fulfill, which will lead to the fulfillment of everyone. If you realize that no matter what people do or don't do (what they *should* or *should not* do) they are always of good intent, then you can let go of "shoulding" them.

The next step is to become more aware of your own "shoulds," for they are clues to your ideals. By bringing your "shoulds" to conscious awareness, you can also get to know your ideals better. And by getting to know your ideals—recognizing what values are behind your "shoulds"—you can begin monitoring your growth toward those ideals, and you can consciously cultivate habits of mind that will help you get there.

Exercise

1. Here is a list of everyday actions people take. After reading each item, think about whether you approve of the action, disapprove of it, or feel neutral about it. For those actions you approve or disapprove of, think, "What kind of person would do this?" Consider the ideals and beliefs you hold about those ideals that are revealed by the answer to this question. Next, ask yourself whether your beliefs help you or hinder you in your progress toward these ideals. If they hinder you, what beliefs—habits of mind—can you cultivate to enhance your progress?

   a. Smoking cigarettes
   b. Doing community service
   c. Answering back
   d. Helping your children with their homework
   e. Ignoring a plea for help
   f. Making fun of someone
   g. Being a vegetarian
   h. Gossiping
   i. Being on the honor role
   j. Choosing to get a divorce
   k. Going back on an agreement
   l. Telling your parents what they don't want to hear
   m. Having sex without love
   n. Being homosexual
   o. Being polite
   p. Pretending you know something you don't
   q. Saving money
   r. Feeling passionately sexy
   s. Making people wait for you
   t. Keeping a secret
   u. Being kissed in greeting by an acquaintance
   v. Slamming the door in someone's face
   w. Yelling at your mate
   x. Praying
   y. Swearing
   z. Being loyal to your country

2. What are the attributes of the ideal:

   a. female
   b. male
   c. mother
   d. father
   e. son
   f. daughter
   g. sister
   h. brother
   i. wife
   j. husband
   k. lover
   l. worker
   m. learner
   n. healer
   o. meditator
   p. housekeeper
   q. leader
   r. soldier
   s. citizen

Do you see any conflicts? For instance, can you work toward your ideal in the role of male/female while also working toward your ideal in the role of lover? Or toward your ideal in the role of leader while also working toward your ideal in the role of son/daughter? Do the attributes of one ideal role conflict with the attributes of another? If so, what new habits of mind do you need to develop?

Habit of Happiness #5

First of all, when you find yourself "should-ing" someone else, stop it! Realize that it is *your* "should" and that it reveals *your* beliefs about a certain ideal or set of ideals. Look for those beliefs. Next, notice when you're using such beliefs to put yourself down or to make yourself wrong. As soon as you notice this, tell yourself that you are always growing closer to your ideal, and that any failure is a lesson for you, a reminder, a gentle nudge in the right direction. Pat yourself on the back for your progress.

6

Mass Beliefs

Beliefs are quite different from ideals. Rather than goals to strive for, they are basic statements we continually make to ourselves about what we consider to be true here and now, what we really *expect* of reality. They are the way we habitually view the world—our habits of mind. All of us must have certain beliefs in order to exist in this reality; we have telepathically decided that these beliefs are the rules of the game, the focus of the drama. Seth calls such beliefs root assumptions. Space and time are both root assumptions: Everyone perceives this reality as based on a series of moments in time and dimensions in space. There are a number of beliefs like space and time that keep us operating in three-dimensional reality. On the other hand, we have many other beliefs—habits of mind—that seem to us to be just as basic but which actually are not: They are not the necessary, agreed-upon rules to live by that we take them to be. But many of these beliefs are so pervasive and widespread, so habitual with so many people, that we never question them; they seem to be true statements about reality and to be the *only* true statements. Some of these beliefs are held by an entire culture.

While each of us is a playwright—writing, producing, directing, and starring in our own unique dramas—we also cooperate with others in creating enormous epics with millions of players, trying out our beliefs en masse in order to see what the material world looks like wearing them. Once we have learned as much as we can using one belief system, we change the set of assumptions and see what new possibilities we can come up with using *them.*

In fact, the history of mankind is a history of fluctuating belief systems, in which various cultures agree to certain ideas about the nature of reality for a time, basing their educational systems on this view of reality, which, of course, strengthens the belief system and prevents other conflicting ideas from entering. The system works well for a while, and those involved all learn a lot about their collective beliefs by viewing them on display "out there." But, inevitably, some of the people in the system experience certain phenomena that cannot be explained under the prevailing system. This is so frightening to the establishment that for a long time these incidents are swept under the rug or otherwise explained away. But after a time along comes a genius, respected by the establishment, who comes up with a solution to the dilemma that is so powerful in its ability to link together all of these unexplained events, and so far-reaching in its consequences, that it then becomes more important for the keepers of the system to explore the implications of this "heretical" notion than it is to protect the belief system from breaking down. And so, over a period of time, the old belief system does break down and is superseded by a new one based on the view of reality foreseen by the genius.

The Western world is presently experiencing such a paradigmatic shift—the disintegration of an old belief system and its replacement by a new one. And the genius who precipitated this shift was none other than Albert Einstein, who, more than eighty years ago, stated the unthinkable when he said that space and time were *not* absolute and independent but relative to each other. This idea went against all of the established Western ways of looking at the world, against all of the old habits of thought, against what we *knew* reality to be, and yet it explained a lot of things that had puzzled scientists for years and suggested new theories that it would not have been possible to formulate before. So it was accepted into the system. And since that time, other ideas which were once considered totally untrue if not outright insane have slowly made their way into the system, creating a receptive environment—a receiving station—for more new ideas of that sort. The Seth material is an important example of these new ideas.

The next hundred years, then, will see the completion of a revolution in thought—the establishment of new habits of mind—that began more than eighty years ago with the Theory of Relativity. But the Western world is still dominated today by the old belief system, the old habits of mind. It takes a long time for an entire society to give up beliefs that they have held for centuries, beliefs that to them are *facts,* which they act upon habitually without ever questioning them. All of you reading this book are showing yourselves to be open to the new ideas coming into the emerging belief system, becoming aware of many potential new beliefs; however, most of you are probably not aware of many of the old beliefs, the old habits of mind, under which you still operate. For these old beliefs are hidden from you, are habitual, taken for granted as facts about the world, and are not viewed as beliefs that can be changed.

But before we look at specific examples of how our thinking is dominated by these old habits of mind let me list some premises of the still-dominant system.

1. Reality is divided into two mutually exclusive parts: the world of the mind and the world of matter.
2. The material world is like a giant clock, existing in empty three-dimensional space and ticking away steadily, second after second.

3. Time is passing; time is running out.
4. The parts of this clockwork world interact in predetermined ways according to certain laws.
5. Our bodies are like miniature clocks within this system, and the parts break down and need repair or replacement every now and again.
6. Every symptom of breakdown can be traced to one cause and to one cure.
7. Without outside intervention this body-machine is helpless.
8. We do not know what mind is or how it works, nor can we ever know, because the only valid approach to knowledge is via the scientific method.
9. The scientific method involves observation, measurement, and quantification, which cannot be carried out with the nonmaterial mind.
10. The mind seems to exist inside the brain, but is not the brain, so as minds we are trapped inside our bodies.
11. Since we cannot know what the mind is or how it works, it will forever remain an unfathomable mystery, a dark repository of images that controls us without out knowing it.
12. On the other hand, we can *develop* our minds (which, when we were born, were blank slates) through our manipulation of the environment.
13. Since we are *not* our bodies and by extension not our environment, and since the environment, like our bodies, is nothing but a machine, we can use it for our own purposes.
14. That purpose is survival.
15. We have no other purpose in life than to survive.
16. Those who ascribe meaning to life are not rational thinkers, but intuitive thinkers, and rationalism and the scientific method are the only ways to truth.
17. Intuitive thinking is feminine and therefore weak.
18. Feminine values—passivity, receptivity, cooperation, intuitiveness—are inferior.
19. Masculine values—aggressiveness, expansiveness, competitiveness, rationality—are superior.
20. Therefore our academic, political, and economic institutions must be founded on masculine values.
21. The better we manipulate our environment, as compared to other people, the better we will survive.
22. It's dog-eat-dog; every man for himself.
23. The more we consume and the more we accumulate, the higher our standard of living will be.
24. The higher the standard of living we have, the better off we are compared with others: The more we prove our survival ability, the better and more powerful we are.

25. The more power we have the better.
26. More is always better.
27. Since *everyone* wants power and since everyone is out to get more power, we've got to be very careful in protecting ourselves.
28. We have to make sure no one takes any of our power away, be it possessions, an opportunity, or a job. We must protect ourselves from people out to get something from us.
29. And we've got to watch out for other countries, too, for some of them are big and powerful, perhaps as big and powerful as we are, and if we don't protect ourselves, if we don't make sure we can defend ourselves, then they will surely take advantage of us.
30. And we have to make sure the little countries without power are on our side, because their being on the other side gives the other side more power.
31. "They" are all out to take advantage of us, looking for a way to exploit us and thus gain more power.
32. We never have enough power.
33. We never have enough of anything!

I have, of course, listed here only some of the beliefs of the old system, and all of those listed are negative, limiting ways of viewing the world. There are many positive beliefs we have gained from the old system as well, but since they give us no trouble, I haven't mentioned them. Now, I am sure you have heard these ideas before and probably, as far as you're concerned, you consider most of them to be totally alien to your belief system. You *know* you don't believe in a clockwork universe, you *know* you don't believe in exploiting your environment and other people, you *know* you don't believe in a dog-eat-dog world. Perhaps this is still the prevailing world view of this culture, but you just don't buy it. Right?

We create our reality through our beliefs, as Seth says over and over again. There isn't one thing that we do or say or feel that isn't in some way a reflection of our beliefs. The trouble is what we *say* we believe and what our true habits of mind are are often two different things. For instance, say you profess a belief in equality, and yet "out there" in the "real" world you see many examples of inequality. If you really did believe in equality, instead of having it as an ideal you are aiming for, then you would create equality, not only in your personal life but also in all situations you were involved with. By the same token, if you believed in peace, peace would surround you. But if you *say* you believe in peace and experience unrest, then you only *wish* you believed in peace; you have a hidden belief—a habit of mind—opposed to bringing you that wish.

I am not saying that hidden beliefs are necessarily bad, for we all have a great number of beliefs we are not consciously aware of that serve us well. But if you have a hidden belief that prevents you from having what you consciously desire, don't you want to become aware of it? Don't you like to feel you have a conscious *choice* in what you believe?

The following exercise is designed to help you discover beliefs you have that are related to the mass beliefs listed above.

Exercise

Choose five of the beliefs from the list on pages 33 to 35. Be intuitive about your choice: Trust yourself to choose those beliefs that will lead to important insights about yourself. Now answer the following questions for each of the beliefs.

1. Do you *expect* this belief to be a part of your reality at least sometimes? When? Under what circumstances?
2. What emotions, memories, or experiences have you had that support this belief?
3. Do you see this belief as true of the world "out there" or of other people but not of yourself?
4. Do you want this belief to be a habit? If so, why?
5. If not, what small steps can you take that will support a more positive belief, that will develop a new habit of mind?
6. How can you use your imagination to aid this process?

Habit of Happiness #6

Notice yourself thinking habitually. Use what you have learned from the exercise in this chapter to help you bring to conscious awareness those habits of mind you want to get rid of. *Don't judge;* simply observe yourself thinking habitually.

7

Actions as Reflections of Beliefs

I am going to cite a couple of common examples of actions people take that reflect beliefs—habits of mind—they may not know they have, beliefs that are held en masse. The fact that almost everyone holds these beliefs makes them all the more hidden, for there are rarely other points of view with which you can compare your own.

The first example is locking everything up. Do you always lock your car when you park it somewhere? Why do you do this? Because, you'll probably say, if I don't someone might steal the car or take something from it. Doesn't this action reflect a belief in the world as a hostile, dog-eat-dog place?

Wait a minute, you say. I don't believe in ripping anyone off, but how can I stop others from doing it? Rip-offs happen all the time. How can I counteract the beliefs of all those people "out there"?

Remember the radio station analogy in which we attract (and are attracted to) those beliefs that fit into our systems? Well, this is an example of the analogy in action. Though you do not believe yourself to be a person who rips people off, you do believe that there are people out there who might rip *you* off. You send this belief out and like a magnet it attracts to it those people who believe in ripping others off. They are attracted to your belief, and your belief is attracted to theirs. A fit!

I guarantee that if you really didn't believe you'd get ripped off, you wouldn't. You simply wouldn't attract to you people who believe in ripping off others, and you wouldn't experience the hostile world that this belief supports. I'm not saying stop locking things up all of a sudden if you have been doing so for years because the habit of mind is well ingrained, but you could start by not locking the car all the time and see what happens. In this way you could gradually build toward a new habit of mind supporting a friendly, cooperative universe where rip-offs don't happen.

I have a dear friend who is a serious student of the Seth material. In fact, she gave some *Create Your Own Reality* workshops using my workbook. For the many years that she lived in Berkeley, she firmly believed that the world was a safe place. She never locked her car (leaving her keys on the floorboards) and she never locked her house. She had never been robbed.

Then she moved to Los Angeles. Within six weeks she got ripped off three times. Twice someone rifled through the glove compartment of her car, which was unlocked, as usual. And once someone came into her unlocked apartment and took her stereo and a camera. She came to me gravely disturbed. Here she had always believed in the world being a safe place, but now that belief wasn't working for her. Her faith was shaken, for this seemed to indicate that she didn't create her own reality entirely. There *was* a world "out there" happening to her over which she had no control, and her beliefs didn't protect her from it.

"How would you describe L.A.?" I asked her.

Well, she couldn't find enough negative things to say about the place. All the people she'd met were phonies, she felt, pretending to be something they weren't. She didn't trust them, and she felt their hostility wherever she went.

Once she had voiced these beliefs, she could, of course, see why she had created the (new) reality that she had. Her belief in the world being a safe place had been limited to a *particular* world. Within that world where she believed herself to be safe she had created safety for herself. But when she went out of that realm into different surroundings with strange people (according to her accustomed standards), she didn't know what to expect, and rather than welcome the unexpected, she feared it: She didn't believe she was safe anymore. Thus, she created that reality for herself, one in which it was unsafe to leave her possessions unlocked.

I've used this particular example because it illustrates a common tendency among people I've known to believe they create their own reality—up to a point. But then, when the "unexpected" happens, when something goes against what they *think* they believe, they do not reexamine their beliefs but instead use the incident as proof that we only create our reality up to a certain point. After that, it's out of our hands.

The point is, our beliefs do change from time to time and place to place—sometimes from one day to the next and from one block to another. In certain situations our beliefs are positive, and for this reason so is our experience. In others our beliefs are negative, creating a negative reality. It is *not* the other way around: Our reality does not create our beliefs; our beliefs create our reality. This point cannot be emphasized enough. Knowing this frees us to change our reality when we don't like it. Not knowing this sentences us to repeating the same negative experiences until we *do* know.

Let's take another common example of actions that reflect mass beliefs: health insurance. Do you have health insurance, or would you if you could? The mass belief behind taking out insurance on your health is, of course, that the body is an object, a machine that needs outside intervention to keep it running, instead of as a self-regulating, self-sustaining, dynamic organism of which your mind is a vital part. And has it ever occurred to you that the only way you can get your money's worth out of health insurance is to be sick at least enough to get back the money you put in? Of course it is a real coup if you can have a long, serious illness, perhaps a major operation and a hospital stay, for which the insurance company must pay. Then you're really making out! To buy health insurance is to bet against your own health. The insurance company is betting you'll *not* get sick, and you're betting you will. It seems to be a no-win situation. On the other hand, if your mental habits in this area are firmly established, and you fear incurring a huge medical bill you cannot afford, then by all means buy health insurance. But be aware of the belief underlying your action and know that a belief in your own good health is the best possible "insurance" you can have.

Exercise

For each of the actions listed below write the beliefs that you see underlying them. Ask yourself whether you have these beliefs—habits of mind. If so, ask yourself if they limit you. Ask yourself whether you accept those limits. If you do, ask yourself why. We often choose to put limitations on ourselves in order to learn from them and perhaps to free us up in other ways. If you don't accept those limits, ask yourself what new habits of mind you can form that will lead to different actions. What would some of these actions be?

1. Taking part in antiwar demonstrations
2. Having an unlisted phone number
3. Taking primal-scream therapy
4. Going on a diet
5. Installing a burglar alarm
6. Keeping a month's stock of groceries
7. Spending your paycheck the same day you get it
8. Making fun of psychics
9. Carrying a handgun
10. Sending aid to the contras
11. Meditating
12. Taking a course in nutrition

Habit of Happiness #7

Be aware of the beliefs underlying your actions. Think of new habits of mind to replace those beliefs you find too limiting. Envision acting on these new beliefs.

8

Emotions as
Reflections of Beliefs

Most people tend to make a big distinction between thoughts (beliefs) and emotions. Thoughts are in words, which makes them concrete and thus "rational"; emotions are wordless feelings, ephemeral and "irrational." Some people look down on emotions, which, in keeping with the prevailing mass belief system, are regarded as feminine and weak. They see thoughts—words, ideas, beliefs—as rational, masculine values and therefore superior. After all, thoughts are the main tools of the scientific method, and the scientific method is considered the only valid approach to knowledge under the dominant belief system.

Emotions tend not only to be looked down upon (and not just by the logical empiricists of our culture: Buddhists, for example, consider the emotions to be an obstacle to enlightenment) but also generally to be considered uncontrollable. They "just happen." A child "just happens" to be afraid of the dark; an adult "just happens" to be afraid before appearing before a large audience. It almost seems at times that our emotions *cause* our beliefs; first we are afraid and then we see something "out there" that is fearful, that we believe endangers us. It seems that we form this belief because of our emotions.

But as Seth says over and over again, it is always the other way around: We have a belief, which generates an emotion. If we believe something is dangerous, then we feel afraid. If we believe something is safe, then we feel unthreatened. From this viewpoint, the distinction between thought and emotion breaks down: Emotions can be seen as symbolizing beliefs. In fact, you could say that beliefs—or, rather, the words that formulate the *essence* that is belief—are one way to symbolize that which comes from the inner world, and emotions are another way. Words and feelings, then, work together in order to symbolize our inner world "out there." They are two different aspects of the same thing.

For the most part, though, even for those of us who may put a higher value on being a rational, thinking-oriented person, and a lower value on being an intuitive, feeling-oriented one, we are more *aware* of our emotions than we are of our beliefs. This, obviously enough, is because we *feel* them. We don't feel thoughts, beliefs, or words. We do feel emotions, especially when the feeling is an uncomfortable one: It is easy for a pleasant state to go unnoticed, but it isn't so easy to ignore an unpleasant one. This is precisely why the emotions serve as valuable clues to our hidden beliefs—particularly mass beliefs—which make us unhappy, which limit us unnecessarily.

If we can learn to look behind the unpleasant emotions, which are so apparent to us, to the beliefs that they symbolize, which are not so apparent, we can discover a lot that we may not find out from simply asking ourselves whether or not we believe this or that. For, as we have seen, often what we think we believe we don't really believe. We want to, but we don't. However, what we *feel* is unmistakably either pleasant or unpleasant. If we think we believe, say, in a peaceful, cooperative universe, yet we find ourselves, instead of feeling good, feeling bad—fearing to walk the streets of our cities at night, for instance—we can be sure that what we think we believe is not what we really believe. Our feelings always tell us the truth about our beliefs. In this sense they are like helpful friends to us. All we need do when feeling frightened or angry or depressed is ask ourselves what is behind the emotion, and we discover beliefs we weren't aware of, which may go against what we thought we believed.

Let's take the emotion of stage fright as our example. What belief—habit of mind—do you suppose is behind this unpleasant feeling? I think it may be a belief that you will be ridiculed or that you will "make a fool" of yourself or that you will otherwise incur the displeasure of your audience. These beliefs are specific examples of the prevailing mass belief that the universe is hostile, the belief in "every man for himself" in competition; it is quite the opposite of a belief in a cooperative, unified, interacting, supportive universe that the emerging world view (and the Seth material) promotes. It can take a long time to move outmoded or undesirable habits of mind out of our systems and to replace them with others that are more desirable if we're not aware of the beliefs that still linger there. Becoming aware of a belief or habit of mind is the first step in getting rid of it, and sometimes the only step necessary. You might say to yourself, "Aha! Thank you, friend emotion. Now I see that stage fright is based on a belief in competition and separation. Isn't that unreal!" And the next time you give a presentation you may not have stage fright. It can happen that way.

In any case, it is important not to go into combat against those beliefs you want to get rid of. If you believe that you must go to war with yourself in order to eradicate your old beliefs, you will, of course, only cause a war within yourself. Instead, realize that all of your beliefs have had a purpose in your life, and that they may have served you well at one time. Make it okay for them to exist and for you to have them. Do not focus in on them with great concentration (which serves continually to activate them; as Seth says, you get what you concentrate on); instead, adopt the attitude that now you have discovered the reason for your negative feelings you can practice having another belief that will bring more desirable results. Then practice the new belief. Keep it in your conscious mind. Say it over and over again, or better, write it down. Notice how you *feel* when you think of that new belief and get used to putting the belief and the feeling together. Use your imagination, which, with dreams, is one of your greatest reality-creating tools, to put you in situations where you operate under this new belief and feel its results. Before long you will begin to find the reality outside of your dreams and imagination reflects this new belief back at you.

Exercise

After reading each situation listed below, think about whether it feels pleasant, unpleasant, or neutral to you. Then, for each item that feels unpleasant, ask yourself what beliefs underlie the emotion. Ask yourself if you want to keep these beliefs and, if so, why. If you don't want to keep these beliefs, think of other more positive habits of mind. Imagine the feelings you would have if you acted according to these new habits.

1. Asking for help
2. Helping
3. Taking care of
4. Being taken care of
5. Announcing something that's important to you
6. Comparing
7. Being challenged
8. Telling off someone
9. Being unable to choose between possibilities
10. Having someone try to lay a guilt trip on you
11. Tidying up
12. Showing off
13. Seeing someone do something well
14. Seeing someone get laughed at
15. Being publicly honored
16. Keeping a secret
17. Trying to be diplomatic
18. Looking for housing
19. Coming into a new group
20. Trying to convince somebody of something
21. Being puzzled
22. Being alone
23. Having to meet a deadline
24. Reprimanding a worker
25. Being on welfare
26. Applying for a job

Habit of Happiness #8

Use your emotions as friendly guides to your beliefs. When you experience an unpleasant emotion, ask yourself what belief underlies it. Often, doing this is enough to make you feel better, for you realize there is a *reason* for your feelings—they didn't come out of nowhere. Try to change those beliefs you don't want to have by imagining yourself with more positive beliefs. *Feel* their effect on you. Connect the positive belief with the positive emotion and imagine yourself in various situations thinking and feeling in this new way.

9

Memories as Reflections of Beliefs

Do you feel you have had a hard struggle in life? Another clue to hidden beliefs—habits of mind—is memories. This may seem strange to you, but what you remember about the past is a reflection of your present belief system. Seth makes this very clear. If, for instance, all or many of your memories are of struggle, then you believe *here and now* that life is a struggle. And certainly the prevailing world view of this culture would back you up. But, you may protest, look at all the hardships I have been through in the past. It *was* a struggle, and that's a fact! That doesn't necessarily mean that I think life is a struggle *now* and will continue to be. I'll grant you that perhaps I believed in struggle in the past, but that doesn't mean I believe it now.

But it does mean you believe it now, for you wouldn't attract those ideas about the past to you now unless you believed in them now. Remember that radio station? Well, many of the thoughts flowing by your antennae are of the past, and you only attract to you (and are only attracted to) those thoughts that are compatible with your *present* belief system. Only those thoughts that are significant to you, that you expect to happen, that fit in with your other mental habits are drawn into your system and then used in creating your present reality. By dwelling on memories of past struggle, by habitually thinking in terms of struggle, you recreate it in the present.

Let's say that you were very poor when growing up and had to work very hard, and that at the time you got into the habit of thinking of life as a struggle. Let's add that you are now no longer poor; you have a well-paying, pleasant job. And yet something is missing. You had thought that once you had money everything would be different. You know you're no longer struggling . . . and yet . . . you still think in terms of struggle and bring struggle right into the present where it takes another form: worry, unease, a sense of disappointment. So the struggle goes on, and, in a way, it is more difficult than the previous struggle because it is more subtle and confusing.

On the other hand, suppose you once were poor and had to work hard and you believed life to be a struggle. But now you are no longer poor, have a pleasant job, and have given up the habit of believing in life as a struggle, replacing it with a belief that life gets better and better. Your memories will reflect this new viewpoint! You might recall incidents from the past that would have been interpreted as illustrating life's struggle in the first example, but from your present perspective they would be interpreted as stepping stones up to where you are now—each step you found yourself on being better than the last. What I'm saying (and what Seth has said many times) is that you will not only choose to remember incidents from the past that support your belief system now but also interpret past events in accordance with your present belief system. So, use your memories as clues to your present habits of mind.

Remember, though, that our beliefs fluctuate from time to time and place to place (as I mentioned in chapter 7), and because of this our emotions and memories also fluctuate. Have you ever noticed that when you're feeling good (when you have positive beliefs operating) you also have pleasant memories? That you recall incidents in the past that evoke similar feelings (based on similar beliefs)? For example, none of us *always* believes that life is a struggle. It is only under certain circumstances that some of us believe this, and once we can get the beliefs out into the open, using our actions, emotions, and memories as clues, we can then look at the circumstances under which we have this belief. One way to cut down on the times this belief is activated, then, is to reduce the circumstances under which we have it.

As a matter of fact, we tend to do this automatically. We all want to feel safe, so we set up our lives in such a way that we do—a lot of the time. And the more aware we are of those circumstances under which we feel unsafe, we can, in many cases and if we so desire, cut down on them. For instance, to use the example from chapter 8, we can decide not to give any more speeches before a large audience and thus avoid the unpleasant feeling of stage fright, which will cut down, as well, on unpleasant memories. We can rewrite our play!

But ultimately, avoiding experience is not the answer to leading happy lives. Our idealistic nature craves the challenge and learning that come with new experiences, so that if we avoid one experience we will create another in its place designed to help us to learn and grow. It may work sometimes—at least in the short run—to stop doing certain things that activate our negative beliefs, but usually, in the long run, it is better to work directly to change the beliefs (while perhaps temporarily suspending some particularly nerve-racking activities). For when you change your beliefs, your reality, with all of its events, will also change: You will no longer need the lesson/challenge that certain circumstances (and you as playwright) have set up.

Besides being clues to our present beliefs, memories can also serve to bring into the present our positive beliefs (and feelings) from the past. Say you are down on yourself about something you've done, remembering other times when you did the same thing. You can, with conscious effort, bring to memory times in the past in which you behaved well, when you felt good. By focusing on these good memories you evoke the beliefs that went with them and bring them into the present along with the pleasant emotions associated with them. We have already seen this in chapter 3.

To summarize, our memories are helpful to us because they reflect our present state of mind—the beliefs we are holding right now. They go along with and support our belief system. Through our memories we can see the circumstances under which certain beliefs have been present. And through our memories—through deliberately evoking positive ones when the present feels negative—we can bring some of our positive beliefs, which have worked well for us in the past, into the present, and thus begin building a positive future for ourselves.

Exercise

Answer each of the questions listed below. Then consider what beliefs these memories reflect. What circumstances cause you to believe, feel, or remember this way? What pleasant memories do you have to help you replace these negative beliefs with positive ones?

1. What unpleasant memories do you have that are associated with your parents and early years of life?
2. What unpleasant memories do you have that are associated with your teachers and school years?
3. What unpleasant memories do you have that are associated with your employers, employees, and work?
4. What unpleasant memories do you have that are associated with your friends and peer activities?
5. What unpleasant memories do you have that are associated with your loves and sexual activities?
6. What unpleasant memories do you have that are associated with marriage/divorce?
7. What unpleasant memories do you have that are associated with your creative efforts?

Habit of Happiness #9

Be aware of what you remember and see how that reflects and supports your present beliefs. Notice the circumstances under which you have tended to believe this way. When you experience negative memories/beliefs, evoke memories reflecting positive beliefs and see how good this feels!

10

The Future as a Reflection of Beliefs

When you envision the future, do you generally feel good about it or apprehensive? Do you look forward to it or dread it? How much do you worry about whether or not something is going to happen?

Our memories reflect our beliefs, and so, too, do our thoughts of the future. What we believe right now we project into the future and *expect* to happen. I know a woman who is always late to gatherings of any kind. Her friends have come to know this about her and try to work around this trait. If they are planning a dinner party, for instance, they will invite Deborah to come an hour earlier than they plan to serve dinner. The other guests will be given the correct time. This way, everyone arrives at the same time; the hostess doesn't feel irritated about having to hold up dinner, and the other guests aren't annoyed because they're hungry and Deborah hasn't arrived yet.

But Deborah is an active person in her community and attends many events open to the general public. She is always at least half an hour late for these, which often disrupts the proceedings and usually elicits at least one hostile comment from a prompt citizen who resents latecomers. She has been told a number of times by a number of people that they don't appreciate her attitude, which seems frivolous or uncaring to them. They feel she lacks respect for, or commitment to, the various projects she is involved in.

But from what I know of Deborah, she is a very caring and committed person, a hard worker who puts a lot of time and effort into whatever she undertakes. She can always be relied on to carry out any tasks she agrees to do. In most ways she is the ideal community member—except for this chronic lateness. She used to tell me how she wished she could "get over" her annoying habit and that she had tried hard to be on time for various occasions but had always failed.

One time I asked her, "What is it you think about when there is an event coming up within, say, twenty-four hours that you are planning to attend?"

"Well," she answered, "the first thing that comes to mind is that I don't want to be late for it. I am always worried that despite my best intentions I'll somehow end up being late again and people will be annoyed. I don't like them to be annoyed, so I don't like being late, but it always seems to happen. I just don't know what I can do to change this bad habit of mine.''

I see Deborah as expressing at least three beliefs about herself here that then become self-fulfilling prophecies. The basic one in this discussion, of course, is that she will be late in the future. She has a lot of "evidence" to back this belief up: She is (in the present) late every time she goes to any meeting. She believes herself to be a person who is late. The second belief is that people will be annoyed. This, too, has happened enough times so that it seems to Deborah to be a fact of life: People will be annoyed at her for her lateness. And the third belief is that she doesn't know what to do about being late. She says she has tried to change and it hasn't worked. This strengthens her belief in not knowing what to do about it. These are her current beliefs and she is laying the groundwork for her future self to "inherit" them through worrying, through concentrating on this "defect," and through repeating over and over again her belief in her incurable lateness. If she were asked to describe what she thinks she will be like in five years, I'd be willing to bet she'd see herself as still being late to everything, with people still annoyed at her, and Deborah unable to do anything about changing.

In chapter 9 we saw how someone can use "evidence" from the past in order to support a belief in the present—in that case, a belief that life is a struggle. In the same way one can use past happenings to create a similar *future* reality. Deborah used *past* lateness not only to support her belief that she is a person who is late now but also to project into the *future* a belief in (expectation of) herself as a late person. Her ideas about herself in the future are based upon what she believes about herself now and upon what she believes she has been.

Of course, all of us do this to varying degrees. Insofar as we worry, expect, dread, look forward to, anticipate, or envision, we build for ourselves, in the present, a future reality. Insofar as we worry about being late, we create that reality in the future. To the extent that we expect ourselves to be a certain way, we create that reality in the future. What we dread, what we concentrate our fears upon, we create. As Seth has said, our imagination, along with our dreams, is one of the most powerful tools we have in creating our own reality. When we use our imagination to project into the future a self we believe to be defective in any way, we increase the probability of that self becoming a reality in a present yet to come. If we continually envision ourselves being late (a future self arriving at a future party late), then we will prepare ourselves for that event in our present. We will write a play for ourselves in which that happens yet again, in order to give ourselves a chance to learn from that belief.

It is important, then, if we want to go on to new lessons instead of repeating old lessons ad infinitum, to be aware of what images of ourselves and our realities we are projecting into the future. If we want to become a *conscious* reality-creator, we need to monitor what we, our present selves, are saying to us, our future selves.

As Seth has repeatedly said, past, present, and future all exist at the "same time," for time, as we know it, does not exist in the inner world (Seth calls it Framework 2), which is where we glean the raw material from which to create our space-time reality. From this inner/ Framework 2 perspective the so-called present is simply an energy point at which the inner world "breaks through" to "become" the outer world (Framework 1). Our past selves and our future selves are really not "past" or "future" at all but are instead an infinitude of probabilities, a pool of possibilities, of raw material, of ideas. Every nanosecond (but really without any "time" going by at all) we choose to make manifest in the outer world one of these unmanifest ideas. We choose to manifest one rather than another through what we, at that point in the present, believe to be true about our reality.

As we have seen, our beliefs fluctuate from time to time and from place to place—and so, too, does our reality. One moment our reality may be one of peace and joy, and the next, one of confusion and fear. And when we're feeling peace and joy, that is, when we're believing things that evoke peace and joy (and perhaps acting upon these beliefs), our memories faithfully reflect back these beliefs, and the future looks rosy. Quite the opposite is true when our beliefs lead to our feeling confused and fearful: Our memories and our future projections reflect those beliefs.

Think once again of the radio station analogy. What happens in the inner/Framework 2 world is that some probable selves—from the limitless pool of probable self-thoughts—those who are most akin to the present (actual) self (who was once probable), are attracted to the antennae, to the broadcast being given. "You," the present self, have attracted them to you through your beliefs, and so they are in your thoughts—your memories and your expectations. These supportive probable selves cluster about your antennae, and attract to them other like ideas to use as more raw material for manifestation. To use the play analogy, they are standing in the wings cheering you on, encouraging you to continue manifesting more of the same, which is attractive to them.

So, when you create your own reality via your beliefs, you also, at every "point in time" create a most likely past and a most likely future for yourself. With every change in belief, the past and the future change too! Now, as mentioned, everyone has embraced root assumptions about themselves in order to coexist in this space-time reality. Thus we perceive of ourselves as coming from the past and going toward the future. The future is what we aim for. Whatever has happened in the past, whatever may be our situation right now, we feel that we must attend to our future if we are to be fulfilled and happy beings.

But this focus on the future can be detrimental, for it takes our minds off the present, *where our future is being created.* Creation always takes place in the present. So, attending to our present and monitoring what beliefs we have right now, which we are sending into the future, along with consciously using our imagination and playfully envisioning the best we possibly can for ourselves, is what will help us create a good future for ourselves.

Exercise

1. Worry is a future-oriented activity, so let's look at some of the things people worry about. What worries do you have about finances, work, relationships, health, creativity, and your psychological well-being?

2. Each one of these worries reflects a belief about yourself *now.* For instance, if you worry about having enough money to get by on in the future, you don't *now* believe you have enough money, or you don't *now* believe you deserve to have money, or you don't *now* believe that you can trust yourself (or the powers that be) to keep money coming in, or you don't *now* want the responsibility for money. Write down the present beliefs that go with the worries about the future you described under number 1.

3. These beliefs may be "justified." For instance, your belief in not having enough money may be supported by the "fact" that you don't have money to buy food and you are starving. Or it may be that you have enough money to eat but not enough for adequate housing. Or you may not have enough to buy a secondhand car, a new car, a second home, or a yacht. Paupers and millionaires can find "facts" to support their beliefs about not having enough money. And by worrying about this "fact," they are setting up a future reality just like the present. In order to counteract this trend, I'd like you to *use your imagination* playfully to envision the best you possibly can for yourself in each of these areas. Consider the topics listed above and write a vivid description of yourself *now* for each of them. Notice the good feeling that comes with each description.

4. Do you find yourself always worrying about certain things? If so, worry has become a habit. Do you think worrying does any good? What would happen if you didn't worry about these things?

5. Visualize (and write down if you feel like it) a scenario in which the you of now goes to meet the you of five years from now. Paint this future you in the best possible light. Make friends with this entity and ask him or her to guide you along the path to becoming this being. Tell him or her you'll stay in touch. Embrace and say good-bye.

Habit of Happiness #10

Monitor your thoughts of the future. Whenever you find yourself projecting a negative belief into the future, immediately change this into a positive idea you want to develop into a belief. Take five minutes every day to imagine your highly evolved future self living a free and happy life. Have a conversation with this self and promise to keep in touch. Embrace and say goodbye.

11

The Body as a Reflection of Beliefs

I know a woman who was seeking a mate through the personals ads. One man who answered an ad she'd put in a national magazine described himself as extremely healthy (among other things). After they'd exchanged pictures and a few more letters and seemed compatible, the man proposed that he fly to see her (they lived in different states) and even named an arrival date. She wrote back to give him the go-ahead, then waited to hear from him. But there was no answer. The arrival date came and went. A week later she got a letter from him saying he couldn't come because "his allergies had acted up . . ."; they had him "at half-mast."

She wondered a bit about the "coincidence" of an allergic reaction happening on the eve of his departure to see her and thought about the Freudian implications of the "half-mast" metaphor. But it soon happened that she had an opportunity to attend a conference near where he lived, so she decided to look him up. She wrote him that she was coming, and he wrote back that he was looking forward to meeting her. When she got to his city, she gave him a call, and they agreed to meet for lunch the next day at a restaurant he designated. She arrived at the agreed-upon time and saw no one fitting his description, so she sat in a booth near the door and waited. After two hours she went back to her hotel. There was a message at the desk to call him at his home.

On the phone his voice was agonized. Taking a shower before dressing to come to the restaurant and meet her, he—an excellent athlete—had "slipped" in the tub and fallen against the rim, cracking some ribs. He was now in excruciating pain and wearing a body brace. Any move he made caused pain.

Well, this was it for my friend. She never met the man, so we can only conjecture about his beliefs. It seems obvious, though, that he was frightened of meeting her, perhaps of meeting any possible romantic partner. At least, he made sure both times they were to meet that he had an "excuse" for not meeting her. This fear was generated by some beliefs he held. One might have been that he was sexually inadequate (the "half-mast" metaphor would indicate this, as well as the fact that he rendered himself impotent—restrained in a body brace, unable to move without pain—before the second encounter). Another might have been that he would be "hurt" by a woman so he decided to hurt himself rather than to let her do so. We will never know for sure, nor does it seem that he will, for he did not seem to be at all in touch with his reality (and thus the beliefs behind it). In his letters he told my friend what he *wanted* himself to be like—his idealized self: extremely healthy and eager to meet a new woman to the point of flying to another state to see her. But if he had really believed these things to be true about himself, they would have met and he would have been healthy.

Remember, we are all playwrights, trying out our beliefs in order to learn from them, and it could be that this man wanted an experience as dramatic as cracking his ribs in order to look finally at the beliefs that prevented him from having what he consciously wanted—a romantic companion. At the same time, my friend was also in this play (her own version of it), and she, too, was thwarted for different reasons—out of different beliefs. Through looking at her beliefs she needs to examine why she isn't getting what she wants.

But I used this example mainly to illustrate how the body becomes a reflection of our beliefs. We create various conditions in the body in order to show ourselves what we believe about many things, or we treat our body in different ways as a result of our beliefs about it. Vegetarianism is an example of this second point.

I have noticed among some vegetarians and other people with special diets a rigidity that is indicative of fear. It may be that the person who took up the diet has been ill a lot, or obese, or weak, or had high blood pressure. That is, in the past the person had a belief in the vulnerability of his or her body, which was reflected in physical reality. Thus the person got in the habit of distrusting the body-mind; he or she did not trust it to select those foods that were best for it. This lack of trust arose out of the "body as a machine" belief. The person didn't have faith in the wisdom of the body but felt that he or she—as a mind separate from the body—had to *protect* the body from all that awful meat and other junk. Now, I'm not advocating junk food necessarily, nor am I advocating that vegetarians go back to eating meat. But I am saying that a good bit of today's food faddism is motivated by a habitual distrust of the body, by a fear of attack from outside forces, by a belief in a hostile universe. Becoming a vegetarian, like buying health insurance, may somewhat assuage that fear, but the belief remains. If you feel the need to convert everyone in sight to vegetarianism I would like to suggest that you ask yourself why. You may be projecting your own fear about your own health onto others, a fear based on a habitual belief in an imperfect, unwise, or helpless body.

The same point can be made about smoking. As a person who enjoys smoking and believes herself to be healthy (and whose body reflects this belief), it is tiresome to be on the receiving end of other people's projected fears vis-à-vis smoking. (Of course, I know that I chose this reality in order to learn from it.)

"But, wait a minute," you say. "It is a *fact* that smoking is hazardous to the health. Look at all the research—*empirical* research—that proves it."

No, it is *not* a fact—it is a belief, a very widespread one, it is true, and one with a lot of negative emotions attached to it. The more advertising about the danger, the more strongly negative the emotions become. But a belief it is—as every single aspect of our reality is a belief, and thus you can choose it or not choose it. I'm not recommending that you take up smoking but only that you recognize that "smoking is harmful to the health" is a *belief* and that underlying this belief is one that our bodies are endangered and helpless machines. Instead of trying to eradicate smoking, try to get rid of that belief, for so long as you continue to have that "endangered body" belief, you will find some way to manifest it. As Seth has said, this increasing outcry against smoking is what is harmful, not the smoking itself, for a lot of people—smokers and nonsmokers alike—are being exposed to this belief, and some will choose to take it into their own belief system and then to make it manifest. Smoking does not endanger your health; believing your health is endangered endangers it!

Epidemics, like wars and other large-scale actions, are a reflection of mass beliefs, of negative mass beliefs in which the body is a metaphor. That the AIDS epidemic first began among homosexuals is not at all surprising. Like cancer, AIDS involves a breakdown in the body's immune system. We are all born with a basic belief in our body's inviolability, and this belief is reflected through the body's immune system. Occasionally, when we have some fears generated by certain beliefs under various circumstances, a virus may make some inroads into the body's naturally protective system, but it is soon stopped. In the case of AIDS, though, the immune system doesn't work, leaving the body vulnerable to any "invader" that comes along. In other words, the AIDS "victim" believes his body is totally vulnerable, and this belief is then manifested in reality.

Since coming out of the closet en masse about a decade ago, homosexuals have been very much in the public eye. Before, they had felt protected by their invisibility; now they are out in the open, being treated with derision and in some cases violence by those members of the straight community who have fear-generating beliefs about homosexuality. (For instance, they may believe themselves to be, at base, gay, and furthermore, to believe that it is unnatural and bad.) In their pioneering attempt to gain respect, some homosexuals are still uncertain about their roles and are trying out different beliefs to see how they look. AIDS no doubt arose out of the beliefs some of them had that they were "bad" and needed to be punished, that they were open to attack and vulnerable, that something was "wrong" with them for being homosexual. That the disease has now spread throughout society indicates that people have chosen to dramatize this belief on a massive basis, not only for themselves to learn from, but also for the world at large to learn from. Value fulfillment again.

Exercise

1. The media use war metaphors when talking about illness: the "crusade" against cancer, the "victims" of AIDS, a virus "invading" the body. What beliefs does such language reveal? Do you think in these terms? If so, how can you change this?

2. What is "wrong" with your body? Make a list.

3. If you were born with some of these "defects," ask yourself why you chose them (for we do create our reality even before we are born). What lessons are you learning from them? Why call them defects if you are learning from them? Can you begin to see them as gifts?

4. If some of these "defects" are ones you chose after you were born, ask yourself why you chose them. What do they do for you? What are you learning? Can you see them as gifts?

5. For those "defects" you want to get rid of, what new beliefs can you develop to replace the old ones? For instance, a common belief of obese people is that they are vulnerable and are protecting themselves from the world through a layer of fat without which they would be open "to attack." What new beliefs could they develop?

6. List any "accidents" you have had in which your body was somehow affected. In each case, look at the events leading up to the accident and those occurring right after it. Can you see what beliefs generated the accident? What beliefs can you replace these with?

7. Think of the illnesses you have had and the circumstances surrounding them. Do you give yourself a cold under certain circumstances? Have you noticed that you always get diarrhea or some other ailment before a stressful event? Does something always seem to "cause" a headache? Do you always get cramps before your period? Do certain things "make you sick"? Ask yourself what beliefs you have that lead you to create these illnesses. Do you want to change them?

8. What do you believe a healthy body is like? Do you have one? Is there anything you feel you need to do (or not do) in order to

attain or maintain health? What would happen if you don't do (or did do) these things? What beliefs are involved here? Do you deserve good health?

9. List at least *fifty* good things about your body.

Habit of Happiness #11

Visualize your body as a vast network of interconnected, cooperative, emotional entities. Take wonder and joy in the intricacy and efficiency of this vast system. Praise your body for the many functions and actions it carries out day after day. Do this daily and *feel* the response from all those entities!

12

Possessions as Reflections of Beliefs

I know a man who has an independent income. Although in some circles his monthly check would not be considered a lot for a single person to live on, in the circles he travels (the woods of northern California) it is considered more than adequate: Many of his acquaintances live on half the amount. By the middle of every month this man runs out of money and has to borrow more to make it through to the next check. Yet, when the next check arrives, he can hardly wait to part with his money again. He buys compulsively, his main passion being car parts and old cars and tools to fix them with. He has a vast array of such items from more than thirty-five years of collecting and is always looking for more and better storage space for them. On occasion he has rented a large garage and ended up in the mechanic business for a while, with people waiting in line to have their cars fixed by him. But he finds this very frustrating because what he really wants to do, he says, is to fix up the cars he has. Still, he never seems to be able to say no to people who need his mechanical expertise, most of whom do not have the money to pay him. So he trades his work for another piece of machinery that doesn't work. On occasion he has managed to find the time to work on one of his projects, perhaps rebuilding an engine for a pickup truck, but he then immediately trades it to someone else for another derelict.

Despite this man's problems in finding storage space for his ever burgeoning collection and his inability to find time to do anything with it, he cannot bear to part with a single item. No rusted old car part exists that he doesn't eventually see some use for—if he can just find the time and the space. Why, just suggesting that he get rid of anything is enough to launch him on a long tirade. His living quarters, which change often, are always so filled with his junk that it is difficult to find a comfortable place to sit, much less have a meal. It sometimes seems that he does not choose a living space for himself but for his junk. He is its keeper, its servant, and its protector; his junk is his raison d'être.

For about ten years now, a woman I know has been barely scratching out a living as an untenured lecturer at various colleges and universities in the highly competitive San Francisco Bay area. Yet you would think she was wealthy from her stylish clothes and from the lavish meals she serves on my frequent visits to her. When we go out for dinner she insists on picking up the tab, and she often gives me little gifts she says remind her of me. On the mantel of her fireplace is an appealing piece of pottery—a whimsical teapot with a smiling head for its lid and two arms gracefully outstretched to form handle and spout. She saw this costly item in an art studio (where her interests frequently take her), and she had to have it. Several payments later, it was hers. This is just one of many artifacts she has on display, all of which make vivid statements about her tastes and interests. She works very hard at her teaching, yet always has time for her many creative pursuits, which include painting, collage making, and ceramics. Much of what she makes she gives to her friends (I have many items). If you admire something she has made, you just may end up taking it home with you—I have seen her gift people in this way many times.

Yet despite all this giving away, my friend always has enough of everything.

These are but two of the many examples that come to mind in which a person's beliefs are reflected through his or her possessions. In both of the cases cited, the people were collectors, but in the first case, the person was coming from a "never enough" belief, holding on to everything he had and not enjoying any of it. He never had enough money; he made sure of this by getting rid of it as quickly as he could. He never had enough time to do what he claimed he wanted to do, his own projects; he made sure of this by "reluctantly" getting caught up in other people's projects. He didn't enjoy his possessions because they needed the work that he never seemed to have time for and because they required space to be kept in. In his dealings with people he always felt ripped off. Even though he would agree to do a job in exchange for merchandise, he would feel unsatisfied after he got it. It wasn't enough!

I see the basic belief underlying all the others this man has in relation to money and possessions as that *he himself* is not enough, is inadequate in many ways, is defective. His old cars and the rusty parts he collects, which he spends most of his money and time on gathering, reflect his self-image of being defective, nonfunctioning, in need of help from "outside." These items, like himself, far from causing him pleasure, cause him hassles, and are a continual reminder to him of what he "ought" to be doing, something he can castigate himself about.

On the other hand, the woman, coming from a "bountiful universe" belief, reflects this belief into her reality. Given how little money she makes as a highly trained teacher, she could, coming from different beliefs, easily complain about her lot in life. But she doesn't *feel* that way; she always finds her world filled with a bounty of things and sees them as extensions of herself—beautiful and elegant and generous. And despite the fact that she works long hours, she always feels she has all the time in the world. She never rushes, and she's always "on time." She uses time and money to her advantage instead of being "taken advantage of" by her beliefs in relation to them.

As we have seen, one of the mass beliefs of the still-prevailing belief system is a belief in scarcity, a belief that we never have enough. On an individual level this belief can lead to the kind of situation just described in which the man carried the belief to a logical extreme, seeing *himself* as not enough. On a mass basis, this belief has led to the creation of scarcity in many areas—depleting natural resources and polluting the environment, for example. Beyond that, it has led to power struggles between nations believing en masse that they didn't have enough power, believing that the other nation might get more than they have. Such a belief, on both an individual and a mass basis, can *never* lead to happiness and contentment. Materially, psychologically, and spiritually, it leads only to strife. But what if we all believed in abundance, like the woman I just described? What if we believed there was plenty of everything for everybody, and we didn't need to strive for more, more, more—that whatever we truly desired would come to us? Think of how different the world would be if that were the case!

Exercise

1. Are you anxious about money? Are you a profligate spender? Are you often overdrawn at the bank? Do you feel you *must* save money? Do you find it hard to save? Does money come easily or has it consistently been hard to come by? Is your *worth* tied to money? Do you feel you have enough money? What are your beliefs in connection with these questions?

2. What do you enjoy spending money on? What do you *not* enjoy spending money on? Do you spend the most money on what you enjoy or on what you don't enjoy? How often do you think about spending money in the future "when you have it" on some item that you "cannot" buy now? Is it always "in the future" that you will "have money"? Do you gift yourself with items or do your gifts always go to someone else? Do you *get* gifts and never *give* them? Are there some items you deserve to have and others you don't deserve? Why do you feel this way?

3. In what ways do your possessions reflect your self-image? What does this say about your beliefs?

4. Which do you enjoy more—giving or receiving? Do you enjoy both? Neither? What beliefs are operating here?

5. Do you envy "rich" people? Do you automatically feel contempt for them? When you see someone driving an expensive car, what do you think about this person? What are your beliefs/feelings about being rich?

6. If you could have everything material you wanted in the world, what would some of these material items be? Why don't you have them now? What does this say about your ideals? What does this say about your beliefs?

7. Try to set aside for a moment the "facts" about reality; set aside all the evidence that continually supports the mass belief in scarcity. Try to imagine what the world would be like if everyone believed in abundance, that they had enough of everything. Describe in detail the way you see such a world.

8. Do you believe a world of abundance is possible? Would you want to live in such a world? Why?

Habit of Happiness #12

Fantasize about having all the material goods you have ever wanted and *know* that you deserve them all. Revel in how good this feels. Take every opportunity to gift yourself, as a symbolic step toward all of this bounty.

13

The Environment as a Reflection of Beliefs

This chapter is an extension of chapter 12, for we have already seen how possessions—which are one aspect of our environment—reflect our beliefs. In this chapter we will look at other environmental aspects, such as living quarters, community, natural (or unnatural) surroundings, friends, other people in your life, and the media. Of all the aspects of your environment, perhaps your possessions seem the most personal to you, yet every aspect is equally as personal in that you have created it through your beliefs, through your desire to see your beliefs manifest in space-time reality.

Let's first take a look at your living quarters. The kind of a domicile you have chosen to live in at this particular time is an important clue to your present beliefs. For that matter, how often you move from one place to another is meaningful, too. I have certain friends who have lived in the same place over a period of many years, while I have moved a dozen times during the same time. This does not at all mean that my friends' realities don't change while mine does but that our attitudes toward moving differ. I know that I have, ever more consciously, used moving from one place to another as a tool in creating the reality I want. My belief is that I will catalyze other changes through changing my environment in this way, while staying in the same place slows down other changes and makes me feel stagnant. On the other hand, I think my friends who haven't moved would say that they have the time and energy to focus on other changes they want to bring about through keeping this aspect of their lives stable. They might also say that by staying in the same place, having that as a given, their other changes, sometimes very subtle, become more pronounced and noticeable. And when they do make a move it's a big deal, a very big change indeed, while my frequent moves, because of their frequency, are not so important.

In any case, staying in one place gives them a feeling of stability while it gives me a feeling of stagnation. Moving a lot would unstabilize them (because of their beliefs) while moving a lot actually gives me a sense of stability—I feel I am growing steadily rather than standing still and "doing nothing to bring about change." But more interesting than one's own particular moving pattern is a change in that pattern. For instance, lately I have been feeling an increasing desire to "settle down." A while back the idea of settling down was depressing to me. Now it isn't. I am getting ready to change my beliefs vis-à-vis stability and stagnation, and soon I will have a different "settled" reality. By the same token, it would be most significant if my "fixed" friends all of a sudden decided to pick up and travel around. It indicates an important change in belief.

What kind of abode a person chooses has a lot to say about his or her beliefs—what it is important to manifest. For some people "security" is very important. Convenience to work is another priority. Esthetics are most important to some. Solitude may be paramount to some people, while economy will matter most to others. Depending on what a "home" means (what your beliefs about it are), you will choose accordingly. Some people cannot stand the thought of living in a condominium, while others wonder why anyone would want to live in a large house. Do you regard your domicile mostly as a repository for your possessions (as in the case we saw in chapter 12), or do you feel intimately involved with it as an expression of yourself, your self-image?

Of course, an extension of your living quarters is the community in which they are located. It is important (in discovering beliefs) not only what type of abode you have chosen but also where it is. Try to look beyond the obvious reasons why you chose a particular community to other more basic ones. For instance, you may say that you chose to live in a particular town because that was where you (or your spouse or whoever) got work. But why did you (or they) choose work there rather than in another place? What were your expectations (beliefs) about that place and what did you want to learn? Asking these questions can help you to uncover some basic beliefs about life and what you want to learn from it.

An extension of the community is its surroundings, whether "unnatural" or "natural." For instance, is it important to you to have a view, and, if so, why? Would you rather the view be a city skyline, a private courtyard, a distant valley, or the sea raging on rocks? All of these preferences say something about the values you are seeking to fulfill for yourself and about your current beliefs about the nature of reality. More important than where you live is whether or not this is what you want for yourself, for this is a book on happiness—on developing habits of happiness. If you are content with your abode, with your community and its surroundings, then you can pat yourself on the back for creating this reality for yourself. But if where you live is where you feel you *deserve to* or *have to* live rather than where you *want to,* then it is useful to look at the beliefs you have that have created this unwanted reality for yourself.

One facet of the surroundings you are in is the climate. Are you a person who likes warm weather but is living where it is cold and rainy much of the time? If so, why are you not letting yourself have what you want? Why are you living in San Diego when you love dramatic changes in climate from one season to the next? If you are dissatisfied with the weather where you live, ask yourself why you are living there.

Friends are a very important part of your environment, and you choose each other to learn about your own beliefs. Most often we choose friends who give support to our own beliefs, but occasionally we choose someone whose belief system is in stark contrast to ours, which tends to make our own beliefs more visible to us. In chapters 15 and 16 we will examine our relationships with friends in more depth, but in this chapter we will mainly look at how our friends reflect our beliefs and values, or how certain friends, because of their very distinct differences in values and beliefs, serve to make ours more visible.

Other people in our lives whom we don't consider friends, such as fellow employees, distant relations, service people we see regularly, and even those we consider to be enemies, are in our play because we have written them into it in order to learn about ourselves. What beliefs do these people exemplify and what do you learn about yourself from them? Why aren't some of these people your "friends"? What is the difference between those people you consider to be friends and those people in your life you don't? Are the people you admire most also your best friends, or is it the other way around? What does this say about your values and beliefs?

For the most part, the media play a more pervasive role in our environment than we realize. It is a rare person indeed who has *no* books, movies, TV, radio, or newspapers in his or her life, even for a short period of time. Are you an avid TV-watcher? What are your favorite programs? What are the beliefs and values reflected to you from these programs? What about TV commercials or magazine advertisements—which ones appeal to you and why? What does this say about your beliefs and values? What kinds of books do you choose to read? What types of movies do you prefer? The answers to these questions can lead to your finding out about some beliefs that you may not be aware of.

Do you find yourself watching the news or other programs on TV night after night and feeling depressed? Realize that you are choosing that reaction. You can instead choose to feel good about what you are viewing, for this gives you an opportunity to see dramatized before you the results of certain beliefs. You don't have to try them out in "real" life in order to learn from them. From this viewpoint, the media are rather like the imagination and dreams: a testing ground for reality-creation.

Exercise

1. What does "home" mean to you? Do you have the home you want? If not, why not? What steps can you take to get what you want in this area?
2. How important is "community" to you? Do your beliefs about home and community clash in any way? Is it possible to have both of your ideals at the same time?
3. Is it possible (according to your belief system) to have the home you want, the community you want, and the surroundings (including climate) you want, all at the same time? If not, why not? Is this okay, or do you want to change it? What beliefs do you need to change?
4. List five of your most important friends. Note why each person is important to you and what beliefs he or she exemplifies. What is that person's role in your life, e.g., helper, informant, lover, sounding board, supporter, leader, etc.?
5. List the first five people who come to mind who are in your life to varying degrees right now but whom you don't consider friends. Note why each person came to mind. What does he or she exemplify? Why is this person not a friend? If you want that person as a friend, why isn't he or she your friend now?
6. What is your favorite TV show? What beliefs do the characters on this show represent? Are these your beliefs as well? If not, why are you attracted to this show?
7. What book, story, article have you recently read that was very interesting? What beliefs were exemplified? Why are you attracted to them?
8. What radio stations do you listen to? How do they reflect your beliefs?
9. What kind of films do you prefer? How do they reflect your beliefs?
10. What are some negative beliefs that you have seen dramatized by the media which you can pat yourself on the back for *not* having?

Habit of Happiness #13

See the many aspects of your environment as reflections of your beliefs—as your own creation. Where you see discord, seek out the beliefs behind it and substitute for them those that reflect harmony. And where you see beauty, congratulate yourself!

14

Your Internal Chatter
as a Reflection of Beliefs

As Seth says, we are all self-hypnotists. By means of our internal chatter, we feed ourselves repeated suggestions that for the most part go unnoticed by our intellect but are nevertheless heard by our "subconscious" and serve as an important source of raw material from which our beliefs are formed. Because we don't often listen to and make ourselves consciously aware of the suggestions we are repeating, when these suggestions become beliefs we aren't aware of the beliefs, either. And in a lot of cases, if we were, we'd be horrified!

I know someone who on many occasions when I was with him has called himself "dummy" because he believed he had goofed up in one way or another. For instance, one time he was driving, made a wrong turn, and said, "Come on now, dummy. You know better than that."

A brilliant scholar I know chooses "stupid" to describe herself whenever she forgets anything. The graceful daughter of a friend uses the word "klutz" to describe what she believes to be awkward moves on her part. A student of mine once said he was "an incurable goofball." "How 'silly' of me" is what my aunt used to say. The list could go on and on.

In all of these cases, I happened to be there when people were talking to themselves. They weren't addressing me but simply blurting out what they thought of themselves at that point in time. These are examples of internal chatter.

Now, I think that if anyone had said one of those things to you, you'd have felt unfairly accused, perhaps insulted. You never like other people laying judgments on you, right? And especially for such picayunish things as making a wrong turn. You know that if you called someone a "dummy" for making a wrong turn or something like that, you'd be in for trouble—or, at the very least, you would not be appreciated.

But we say things like that to ourselves all the time. In chapter 3 I mentioned that we rarely notice our daily doings unless they are either spectacularly successful or in any way seem to be a failure. We take our everyday successes for granted, barely aware of them, focusing instead on our failures. I am sure you have caught yourself from time to time scolding yourself in your mind for something you've done "wrong," and perhaps you became aware of habitually using certain adjectives to describe yourself, such as "goofy" or "silly." Yet how many times have you been aware of mentally praising yourself or of using terms of endearment when you "speak" to yourself? Rarely I would guess. It may have been that the patting-on-the-back exercise seemed strange to you for that reason: You just weren't used to doing such a thing. If we treated our friends and co-workers the same way we mentally treat ourselves, acknowledging few of their successes and all of their failures, we would deserve the lack of cooperation that would come to us.

Think of that. For the most part, we treat even the merest acquaintance with far more respect than we treat ourselves! Thus, one of the best things we can do in terms of developing a sense of self-worth, confidence, and well-being is to get into the habit of noticing and appreciating the many little things we do for ourselves every day. Hopefully by now you are on your way to establishing "patting yourself on the back" as a habit.

In this chapter and for this habit, though, I am going to ask you to look at and get acquainted with those voices within—subpersonalities as they are popularly called—who say things like that to "you." Of course, ignoring these subpersonalities or putting them down for what they say means ignoring and putting down a part of yourself, a part of you who means well and is looking out for your welfare (however misguidedly), just as every other part of you is.

If you want to be a happy person, the single most important habit to get into is self-acceptance. Insofar as you don't accept yourself (all of your selves), you will not accept any of your other creations. There will always be something "out there" to find fault with as long as you find fault with yourself. I will have a great deal more to say about self-acceptance in the chapters to come, but here I want to make the point that self-acceptance does not mean resignation. Accepting yourself completely does not mean resigning yourself to being less than you aspire to be because of your "defects."

Acceptance means saying in each moment that it is okay to be you just as you are; acceptance means understanding why you are doing or feeling or remembering or projecting into the future what you are— by knowing what beliefs you are operating from. Acceptance means seeing yourself as a process, as a person in the state of becoming, whose every action, feeling, memory, and worry, whose body, possessions, environment reflect to you where you are in that process of becoming. Acceptance is realizing that every aspect of your reality can be used as a clue to your beliefs, and so each of these aspects is valuable, for it leads you to ever increasing self-understanding and, therefore, growth. Acceptance means welcoming whatever new disclosures about yourself come to light, for these will help you to *become*.

If you are a good typist, I recommend that you do the following exercise the way I did, visualizing as vividly as possible the subpersonalities involved while typing everything that came to mind as fast as I could, letting the conversation continue without interruption. Another way would be to use a tape recorder and to describe aloud what you are visualizing, and to listen to it later. Dramatize as much as possible; feel your playwright-self appraising these characters and planning a scenario from which all of the parts of yourself can learn.

Exercise

1. Think of a time when you caught yourself in the act of calling yourself "stupid" or another favorite adjective that your subpersonality uses. Now visualize in detail a conversation between the subpersonality who called you that name and "you"—any of your other subpersonalities who does not like being called that name. Have it out. Tell the scolder what you think of him/her for saying such things to you. Then be the scolder and answer this criticism. Say why you called him/her that name, and explain, in turn, how *you* feel about being criticized. Continue the conversation until both personalities have understood and accepted each other's point of view (even if they don't agree). Have them shake hands as friends.

2. Read over what you have written, or listen to your tape, and see if you can pinpoint the beliefs from which each of these subpersonalities is operating. Look especially for conflicts between the beliefs of each personality. For instance, the scolder may believe that anything short of perfection is not okay. The other personality may believe that it is okay to make mistakes. Ask yourself which of these beliefs you want manifested in your space-time reality. Without making the holder of the unwanted belief wrong, see if "you"—as a third subpersonality—can show this personality the advantages of the other belief. Tell him/her that you appreciate the concern shown and say that it is time to move on to new beliefs that will be compatible with the conscious desires of the entire entity. Get that personality to agree to develop that new belief in place of the unwanted one.

Habit of Happiness #14

Befriend your subpersonalities! Welcome each one who comes into the light of your consciousness. Let them have their say, accept where they're coming from, and enlist their aid in developing your habits of happiness.

15

The Beliefs Behind
Approval Seeking

In this chapter and the next one, we are going to be looking at our feelings and thoughts about other people. In chapter 14 we saw that there are many "people" in our head—subpersonalities—who may have conflicting beliefs and thus will be urging us in different directions. Getting to know and accept these personalities, to see what beliefs they are operating from, and then to choose from among all of the beliefs uncovered those that will implement your conscious desires, enlisting the cooperation of all those known parts of the self, is a process that will bring you happiness.

I cannot say too often that *you* create every aspect of your reality. You create the voices in your head in order to learn what beliefs you are operating under at any given time, for, as we saw, beliefs change from moment to moment and from place to place. The voices we hear (if we are consciously aware of them) represent what we believe under certain circumstances. (Of course, we create the circumstances in order to hear the voices tell us our beliefs.) The important point is that we are fluid, ever-changing beings in the process of becoming—not fixed, static products resulting from past experiences. We are always trying out new beliefs in order to learn from them.

However, except under the most dire circumstances (where we may have experienced great self-doubt and fear), at any point in time, whatever beliefs we may be trying out, we can still get in touch with others that we may prefer—this is part of the process. And the more conscious we are of the many beliefs we are testing out, the more choice we have in selecting beliefs that will result in what we consciously desire. Self-understanding (and thus self-acceptance) leads to more conscious choice and therefore more happiness.

In a sense, the people in our lives symbolize the voices in our heads. Since the voices are not "material" and the people are, the people can be seen as material manifestations of the voices within, created by us in space-time (written into the play) in order to afford yet another view of the beliefs we operate under. In *our* play these people are *our* creations; in *their* plays, we're *their* creations. At base, we are all conscious energy getting to know the world from our own unique centers and adding to the overall knowledge and growth of All That Is thereby.

I once knew a woman named Mary who was described by her friends as "an inveterate do-gooder." Few causes came to her attention that she could resist getting involved in. She was always driving people here and there, or going to a nursing home and reading to someone. She never said no to anything anyone asked her to do, often to the point where she was so overextended and so strung out that her friends felt protective of her and would try to shield her from more requests. Usually she'd become ill and have to curtail her activities for a while. When she got well she would start over again.

One of the things I remember about Mary is how agreeable she was to whatever I said. If I thought something was a good idea, Mary did too. If I thought it wasn't, Mary didn't either. More than that, Mary always seemed (from my perspective/belief system) to be pumping me for feedback about herself. She would tell me about something she had done for someone and then look at me as if to say, "What do you think of that?" If I didn't respond to her unstated question it was as if I'd criticized her. She might then ask, "Well, what would you have done?" If I responded by saying I would have done it differently, she was crushed. On the other hand, if I'd say, "That's great, Mary," or something like that, she'd be elated.

Another thing I remember about Mary is that nobody ever seemed to do anything for *her*. This was not because no one tried, but because she seemed unwilling or unable to accept any help from others. If someone offered to give her a ride somewhere, for instance, she'd always say something like, "Oh, no, I couldn't put you to that bother." It was okay that she be bothered to give others rides but not okay for anyone to bother with her.

I once went to visit her in the hospital where her husband took her after a bad cold she got turned into pneumonia. This followed months of her selfless efforts going door-to-door in the ghetto of her city, trying to get people to register to vote. Although she was exhausted and half-drugged, she tried to raise herself into a sitting position and play hostess despite my attempts to keep her prone. She apologized for having the malady that brought me there and protested my gift of flowers. She was worried about her husband being home and having to fend for himself and concerned because she'd not completed her task. I asked her if she had enjoyed doing the voter registration and she confessed that she hadn't—"But someone has to do it . . ."

In chapter 2 I talked about a man who sought approval and self-worth through others. He did this by constantly complaining and insisting that he have everything his own way. His play for getting approval was to force (or to attempt to force) people to notice what he had done and compliment him for it. But even when he did get notice and approval, it wasn't enough, for he still didn't believe he was worthy.

On the surface, Mary appears to be a very different person from the man mentioned earlier. She never complained and, far from insisting on having her own way, she tried to do everything "right"—or what she thought others considered right. Far from forcing people to notice her, she declined any offers of help and apologized for any situation she was in that might put others out.

But despite their behavioral differences, these two people have much in common. They are both operating from similar beliefs about the world, which cause both of them to feel anxious. They deal with anxiety in totally different ways, but the outcome is similar: They never feel satisfied. Whatever approval they get is never enough, for they do not approve of themselves.

Using Mary as the main example here, I see a number of beliefs operating that can only lead to her unhappiness. One of them is that she is dependent on the world "out there" for her approval. She does not believe in her own intrinsic worth but looks to others to define it. This leads to her belief that she must "do good" in order to get approval. She does not trust what feels good to her but looks out there at what "the world" seems to think is good. This makes her very dependent on feedback, and when she gets approval she is momentarily happy: She did the "right" thing. If she doesn't get approval, she feels devastated. Mary believes she is helpless, that she herself doesn't know what is good or bad, and so, when she does something "bad," she not only believes that she herself (not just her action) is bad but also cannot know, the next time, whether she'll be bad again, or good. It's such a relief when she's okay, but she never knows when that will change at the whim of "the world." Mary knows she'd better not be any trouble to anyone or she'll surely not be liked; she'll be looked upon as "bad." The main thing to do is to try as hard as she can to please people and never to cause anyone any hassles if she can possibly help it.

Mary does not see herself or others as individuals, each with his or her own unique values, but sees the world "out there," separate from herself, as one huge, homogeneous, amorphous *judge*. Thus she relates to everyone in the same way: awaiting their judgment, their approval or disapproval. She regards all of the people in her life, her husband, her friends, the people she meets in her many activities, as her critics. Just as she doesn't believe in her own uniqueness, neither does she believe in theirs. Each person's opinion is equally as important, *all* important, to her. She does not discriminate among judgments. And, essentially, she *expects* hostility, for that's the way she sees the world—not as her friend but as her judge.

Few of us are so purely approval seeking as either of the examples cited, but all of us, I would guess, under certain circumstances, seek approval from others. There is, of course, nothing inherently right or wrong with this activity, and a lot can be learned from it—if you're aware of what your beliefs are about it. But if you're not, you don't have a choice as to whether you want to continue such activities or not. The following exercise will help you to get in touch with some beliefs behind actions/feelings that are oriented toward the approval of others.

Exercise

1. Do you like to "show off" on occasion? What are the occasions? Why do you like to do this? Does it feel good? If so, congratulate yourself. If not, what beliefs do you need to change?
2. When you're in a group do you sometimes feel unsure of yourself, worried that your opinions won't be acceptable? If so, how do you handle this? What beliefs are operating? If you want to change them, how would you go about it?
3. How do you feel when criticized? Does it matter who the critic is? What beliefs are operating?
4. Do you have difficulty, generally, in making decisions? Why? How can you change this?
5. What if you say something to someone and he or she doesn't listen? How do you feel? Does it matter who it is? What beliefs are operating?
6. Do you tend to let people think you agree with them even when you don't? Why do you do this? What beliefs are operating?
7. Do you believe everything people say to you about you? If so, why?
8. Do you usually find other people's ideas "better" than your own? Why? What can you do about this?
9. Do you ever make yourself do something you don't want to do? Why? What beliefs are operating?

Habit of Happiness #15

Be your own best friend. Respect your own impulses, actions, and opinions. Realize how unique you are and revel in this uniqueness!

16

Seeing Yourself
in Others (Projection)

A friend of mine, Barry, is a registered nurse and avid photographer. When he first took up this hobby, he regularly borrowed my slide projector, eager to view his latest batch of slides. This was fine with me, except he wouldn't return the machine until I called and asked for it. After he'd done this a few times, I told him I wanted the projector returned promptly from now on (my son was also into photography, and he had dropped by on more than one occasion with a carousel of slides to show—and no projector). The next time Barry went off with the projector he promised he would bring it back the next day, but he didn't. That evening I called him and told him to bring the projector back and that I didn't want him to borrow it any more because I didn't like taking the responsibility for getting it back. He seemed a bit crestfallen but didn't say anything.

A couple of weeks later, one of my cats came home with a gouge out of his back from a fight, and the next day the wound was festering, so I called up Barry and asked him if he could come and have a look at it. He came right over and cleaned and dressed the wound, then said this should be done every couple of days until it cleared up. I made a deal with Barry: If he would come by and clean the wound regularly, he could borrow the slide projector each time. He agreed to this, and left with the projector in hand, promising to come back in a couple of days. Well, you guessed it. He didn't show up, and neither did the slide projector.

Up to this point I had been calm about Barry's repeated failures to keep his word, but this time I was angry. It just wasn't fair, I thought to myself, not fair at all. Here I was, this responsible person who was totally dependable, who always did what she said she was going to do, who always returned what she borrowed, who wouldn't dream of making an agreement and then not following through on it. And what was my reward for this behavior? To have some flake like Barry take advantage of me. It just wasn't fair at all.

Well, I went on for some time feeling sorry for myself and the unfairness of the world, until I caught myself up short. Wait a minute: You created this reality for yourself. What were you trying to learn from it? With that reminder, I calmly sat back and looked at the situation. Okay, what beliefs were operating here? Why was I so angry with Barry? My anger seemed way out of proportion to what he had done. Was it a belief in a hostile world where people get ripped off? No, that didn't seem to be it. I didn't think of myself as being ripped off, only that it wasn't fair, that he could get away with being a flake while I . . . Aha! A new insight. There was a part of me who *wanted* to be a flake, who balked at responsibility, who resisted making or meeting commitments, who didn't like to be dependable, who wished she could get away with behavior like Barry's. I'd never acknowledged this personality before, this part of myself who wanted to be irresponsible, but I had sensed that there was some "danger" that I might become that way. Not consciously realizing that feared part was in me, I projected it "out there" where I could see it in operation. I had created this anger for myself, then, partly out of fear (for anger is fear with aggression attached) and partly out of envy—on the part of that subpersonality who wanted to be just like Barry, who didn't want to be "good" all the time only to see others get to be "bad," who thought it was unfair that Barry got away with such things when she couldn't!

Once I saw this, I could also see how I'd always been hard on myself vis-à-vis meeting commitments, that I'd gone overboard in being dependable and trustworthy. I was *militant* about it—on guard lest my "flaky" side get the upper hand, always watchful of myself that I not behave irresponsibly.

And as I thought further, I realized that lately my life had been filled with irresponsible people: one of my students who never turned in his papers on time, usually with some lame excuse (how scornful I felt!); my daughter who never answered my letters yet who'd call long distance, collect, whenever she felt like it (and without even feeling the slightest bit guilty!); businesspeople who hadn't returned my calls when they'd made a point of saying they would (how could they hold down their jobs!); my neighbor who stayed home from work all day on April 15 in order to get his income tax figured out and mailed by the 12:00 A.M. deadline (when he'd had three-and-a-half months to do it!). Why, flakes had been crawling out of the woodwork around me lately!

Now I could see why. I had written them into my play in order to see what my beliefs in this area looked like projected into space-time reality. They had thus far been invisible to me, so I dramatized them. I dramatized my fear-turned-into-anger, and I dramatized my envy. And once I got in touch with the feeling of envy I discovered "her"—a part of myself who had longed to be recognized, to have a say, a side who felt disowned and dishonored.

Naturally, all of my anger toward Barry disappeared, for it hadn't ever really been directed at him. In fact, I felt so kindly toward him that I called and told him sincerely how sorry I was for being such a grouch about the slide projector. Strangely enough, he returned it the next day without my asking him to and from that time on always returned it promptly. It wasn't that Barry didn't continue to have his own flaky propensities, for when we do our projections we often do them onto appropriate people—people who have something to learn in that connection—but that he thereafter practiced using that trait of his around others; since I no longer needed that lesson, I no longer created that trait in my life. In fact, I no longer thought of people that way. And as time went on I found I wasn't hard on myself anymore about being reliable. Once the conflict within was resolved through the recognition and acceptance of that side of myself who had been fighting, I could relax, for I had "everyone's" cooperation!

Whenever you believe people are "making you" feel a certain way, whenever you believe someone is "preventing you" from doing what you want, whenever you believe you are "being rejected by" someone, whenever you believe that others are "taking advantage" of you, you can be sure you are projecting some beliefs/feelings of yours "out there" in order to find out more about yourself and thus to learn and grow. It is most important to take these projections back and own them, for as long as you ascribe them to "something out there," you will not be able to deal with them in yourself. And if they are not dealt with, they will continue to show up "out there" in increasingly intensified forms until at last you do see the central role you have had in their creation.

Owning your projections means letting go of feeling self-righteous and superior (as I was feeling toward all of those "flakes"), it means giving up feeling martyred and misunderstood, and it means *taking responsibility for your own feelings,* which may be the most difficult feat of all. It means saying to yourself, "I have created this anger I feel through my beliefs. It is not his or her fault that I feel this way, it is my choice to believe this way and to feel this way. That person isn't making me feel guilty: I have chosen this feeling and I can change it." It means letting go of blaming, letting go of feeling sorry for yourself, letting go of jealousy, criticism, suspicion, contempt, arrogance, and prejudice. It means knowing for certain that you very literally and thoroughly create your own reality, *always.*

Exercise

1. Think of a time when you believed someone "made you" do something. What is so "wrong" with that thing you did that you will not take responsibility for it? Is there a part of yourself who wants to be recognized and accepted, who got to have his or her way through that rationalization?
2. Recall a time when you felt "prevented from" doing something you wanted to do. Who was *really* doing the preventing? Why do you need the excuse of "someone out there" who is keeping you from doing it?
3. Under what circumstances do you tend to feel rejected? What part of yourself is doing the rejecting? Why? Can you accept and forgive that subpersonality?
4. When was the last time someone "took advantage of" you? Wouldn't you rather take responsibility for whatever occurred than to feel like a victim? If not, why?
5. Are there some people in your life right now toward whom you feel self-righteous and superior? If so, why? If they have certain traits that you feel superior to or self-righteous about, ask yourself whether you might also have those traits—or opposite traits. If you have opposite traits, are you overcompensating out of a fear of being, at base, like the others?
6. Do you sometimes feel like a martyr? Why do you do that to yourself? Do you get off on it? Wouldn't you rather feel happy? If so, what new habits of mind do you need to develop?
7. Do you feel misunderstood? Can you take responsibility for creating the misunderstanding? What rewards do you get for blaming others for not understanding?
8. Do people lay guilt trips on you? Can you take responsibility for creating your guilty feeling? Why is it *ever* necessary to feel guilty? What payoffs do you get?
9. What "makes" you jealous? Why are you creating this jealousy for yourself—and don't say "I can't help it." Take responsibility for helping yourself!
10. Would you say people are more critical of you or you are more critical of them? The two are related: Insofar as you are self-

critical (whether you recognize it or not), you will either experience criticism from others projected "out there" or you will find yourself critical of others, which is a way of telling yourself you're not okay (just like them) under the given circumstances. Have a talk with your critical self and get him or her to cooperate in forming new habits of mind.

11. Prejudice is *always* projection. People would not have hostile feelings toward others unless they identified with them in some way, through their projections. What are your prejudices? Come on now, you know you're not "supposed to" be prejudiced but you probably are in some way. Own those projections!

Habit of Happiness #16

Take total responsibility for your own feelings! Let go of blaming others for making you feel whatever it is you feel. Look within for that part of you who craves recognition. Welcome and accept that subpersonality.

17

On Forgiving

The single most important habit to get into, if you want to be a happy person, is self-acceptance. I said this in chapter 14 and I repeat it here not only because the concept is of utmost importance but also because self-acceptance and forgiveness are closely related. In fact, they are two aspects of the same thing: To forgive is to accept and to accept is to forgive. For our purposes here, though, I am going to make the following distinction: Acceptance is an ongoing, here-and-now, spontaneous activity, whereas forgiveness is not only that but also a tool to heal the past so that self-acceptance can take place in the present.

Do you have certain memories that persist and keep getting triggered by present circumstances? For instance, you meet someone you feel drawn to, whom you like immediately. But after knowing that person for a short time you find yourself (or him/her) behaving in negative ways that harken back to the past—your behavior (or his/her behavior toward you) in this new situation is the same as it was in the past toward someone else. What you say and do now keeps evoking unhappy scenes of the past.

Or perhaps you have changed jobs; you totally changed your working conditions because you were not happy with them. And yet, after a short time you find yourself feeling and acting *as if* the old conditions prevailed. As different as your new situation is, your feelings and actions remain the same as before and remind you of your former situation.

Interestingly enough, we cannot give up something until we accept it. The more we dislike something, the more bound to it we are, and the more we like it, the freer we are. This especially applies to the past. Whatever in the past we regret, feel sorry for ourselves about, feel bad about the way we or others acted, or in any way feel was negative we hang on to, going over and over it in our minds, and thus revivifying it, bringing it and its negativity into the present, where we act on it once again. On the other hand, whatever we remember with pleasure we do not feel bound by, and thinking of it only refreshes us and makes us feel good and free and happy.

Insofar as we do not forgive and accept ourselves and others, we will keep getting lessons in forgiveness and acceptance. Insofar as we view our attitudes and actions or those of others in a negative light, we will continue to create negativity in our lives. And conversely, once we accept ourselves—different aspects of ourselves, including those we had projected—we are free to go on to new learning in these areas. Once we view various attitudes and actions (which may have *seemed* negative to us once) in a positive light, we no longer find ourselves creating the same situations over again. A negative attitude toward the past binds us to it; a positive attitude frees us from it and creates self-acceptance in the present.

If we don't want the past continually to come back to haunt us, if we don't want to continue repeating the past in the present, we must come to forgive and accept those past selves (and projections) just as we forgive and accept our present ones.

I talked to a friend, John, one day and was surprised to hear that he had split up with his girlfriend, Marsha. They had been living together for about a year and seemed to get along very well. In fact, they had been talking about getting married. All of us who knew John were happy about this new relationship because his previous one, with Melinda, had been so horrible. And it seemed to us that Melinda had been the one who caused all the trouble. In the first place, she had just up and moved in with John, without his asking her or wanting her to. Then she expected him to support her—to pay all the rent and buy all the food and to keep her supplied with dope (she smoked marijuana from morning til midnight). That wasn't all: She didn't do anything around the house. She didn't cook, she didn't clean, she didn't even straighten up things. She just sat around all day and expected John to do all the work. But worst of all was her temper. She was a pretty woman and for the most part very quiet, almost to the point of muteness, which gave her a strangely compelling, mysterious air, until you got to know her. But when she got angry, which was often and always "unexpected," she was like a wild animal, screaming and throwing things, hitting John as hard as she could with closed fists.

John had done everything he could to get her to move out except to throw her out. I think he was always a bit afraid of her. We all wondered how he was ever going to extricate himself from the situation when along came Marsha.

By this time, John was spending most of his time away from his apartment in order to avoid Melinda. He met Marsha at a friend's place, and they hit it off immediately. Marsha could not have been more different from Melinda. The most notable difference was her competence. She obviously knew how to take good care of herself. She had nothing of the waiflike appearance of Melinda. She had been around, traveled a lot, and knew how to talk to people. She had just sold a successful business and was currently "on holiday," as she put it, waiting to see what she wanted to do next.

In most ways, they were an unlikely pair, these two, for John was not at all worldly. In fact, except for one short fishing trip to Mexico, he had never been out of the state. But he had a lot of charm, and it seemed that his humble background and his affinity for the natural beauty of his surroundings appealed to Marsha, who had been living in San Francisco for eight years and wanted to get away from an urban environment. In any case, they fell in love, and, with Marsha's support, John gave notice where he was living and gave Melinda notice. A month later, some distance removed from the ranting, raving Melinda, who threatened to sue John, Marsha and John settled into living together.

And now, a year later, they were splitting up.

"What happened?" I asked John.

The bottom line, he said, was that Marsha just didn't care about him. It was obvious she was using him for her own purposes. Right from the start, after they moved in together, the whole relationship changed. She acted very selfish. She'd get up in the morning and fix a pot of coffee and then she'd sit at her desk and write letters—for hours, sometimes. Or she'd talk on the phone with her friends. She hardly gave him the time of day. Why, often she'd fix herself some brunch about eleven and wouldn't even ask him if he wanted any. And she used to do her own laundry but not do his.

So, he'd get mad at her and tell her what he expected from her, but she wouldn't even listen. She didn't even care. This made him even madder, of course, but then she'd just walk out of the place and come back hours later, all happy from a visit with friends or a hike or a drive. This made him so mad he could hardly stand it.

Then one day she told him she had had it and split. Just like that. He felt totally ripped off. He was going to take her to court or something. To get back at her for what she'd done to him.

This story illustrates many of the ways in which the past can come back to haunt a person. John was hanging on to a number of negatives from the past, which he had failed to learn from: He had failed to forgive and accept himself, and he had failed to recognize, forgive, and accept his projections. And so the lesson was presented again in the present, in a different form, so that he might learn from *this* experience.

As I see it, John had the following negative, limiting beliefs, which led to his creating the reality that he did for both relationships.

1. People are going to rip you off, to use you for their own purposes.
2. If people care about you, they are *supposed to* do certain things for you.
3. Ignoring people, absenting oneself from them, is a way to punish people for something they did wrong.

4. Certain things "make" people angry.
5. Anger is uncontrollable.
6. People are going to reject you—unexpectedly and abruptly.
7. Rejection must be met with revenge.
8. I (John) do not deserve/cannot have a compatible partner.

The interesting thing about this story is that in the first "play" John wrote, Melinda was the lead, acting out most of John's beliefs (which he had projected upon her, a willing target), so that John could see what they looked like "out there." In the second play, John was the lead with *some* of his beliefs, though he still projected "getting ripped off" onto Marsha—quite a feat considering that Marsha's behavior was very different from Melinda's. She was not a willing target for such projections, which is why she left him. In both cases John felt ripped off "by someone." He could not see that it was a part of himself who felt ripped off, who would always feel ripped off as long as its need to be acknowledged was not met. But in the second play, John was the one who expected things to be done for him (cooking, laundry), as Melinda had in the first play. And in the second play John got angry because these things hadn't been done, as we can assume Melinda did in the first play. In both cases, the person at whom the anger was directed was oblivious to what he or she had "done," which is often the case. John found Melinda "unexpectedly" angry; Marsha seems not to have expected John to be angry when she came home from an excursion.

Another reason John was angry at Marsha was that he thought her absenting herself was a way of punishing him, just as his absenting himself had been a way of punishing Melinda (and "making" her angry). It doesn't appear that Marsha really had punishment in mind, but he projected this onto her.

In the second play, John experienced "uncontrollable" anger—getting madder and madder—just as in the first play the anger had seemed uncontrollable in his projection of it onto Melinda. And in the second play, John experienced "rejection," which was unexpected and abrupt to him (despite all the clues), just as it had been to Melinda in the first play (again, with many unnoticed clues). And finally, in the second play, John felt he had to get revenge, just as Melinda had threatened to sue in the first play. He even sought the same mode of revenge—legal action.

This is a case where someone gave himself ample opportunity to learn his lessons. In both plays John had the chance to recognize his rip-off belief, to see that despite the character of the person he was with he still believed he would be ripped off, and from his perspective

he got it. He got what he feared in both cases. And yet he still didn't
get it (the lesson).

He also gave himself the chance to experience anger and rejection
from both sides, and yet he seemed unable to see the parallels between
the two plays. From all John said to me, he did not appear to remember
how he had felt when Melinda had been angry at him, and I would be
willing to bet he did not think of Melinda with empathy when he
experienced his belief in rejection happening to him through Marsha.
Perhaps if he did accept his responsibility in creating both of those
realities for himself, he would then have to contend with the basic
belief underlying all the others, a belief that he doesn't deserve a compatible partner. As long as he could blame others for the incompatibil-
ity of the relationship, he wouldn't have to face up to his basic lack of
self-worth.

It's too bad John didn't learn from all this, for until he does, he
will continue to bring his past into the present. Until he comes to
forgive and accept himself and Melinda and Marsha, until he comes to
recognize and forgive and accept those parts of himself voicing these
beliefs, the internal battle will go on. You cannot let go of the past
until you like it (or, at the very least, *forgive* it)!

Exercise

1. Using John's story as an example, recall two episodes in your past where you experienced similar interactions despite the differences between the people involved. See what beliefs of yours were operating in both cases. Realize that all the characters involved were simply playing their agreed-upon roles in your drama so that you could learn from it. Forgive them and thank them for what they have done for you. They have helped you to learn your lesson.

2. List a number of things you have done that you feel ashamed of. Realize that the past selves who did whatever it was you are ashamed of are not "causing" you the shame—*you,* the present, here-and-now self, are responsible for that feeling, and you are responsible for discovering the beliefs that are generating that feeling. By taking responsibility here and now for whatever feelings you have when you think of the past, you take blame away from those parts of you who acted in the past. This way it is easy to forgive them and even to love them for the lessons they are giving you *now.*

3. List some people you believe have done you wrong. Realize that you chose whatever was done and that you are responsible for whatever feelings you have about it. Forgive them and thank them for their part in your drama.

Habit of Happiness #17

Love your past and welcome your memories. See them as a rich repository of lessons. Take responsibility for whatever feelings you have about people or incidents in your past in the present, where your reality is being created. Forgive!

18

"But, If I'm Happy . . ."

"Growth comes through pain and struggle." "No pain, no gain." "Life is a vale of tears." "I never promised you a rose garden." "You can't have your cake and eat it too." "We all have to pay our dues." "We have to take the bad with the good." "Life always has its ups and downs." "There is no free lunch." "You can't look at the world through rose-colored glasses."

I am sure you are all familiar with the above aphorisms, and many of them you've probably never questioned but taken as a given, as a fact of life. You say, "Of course, it goes without saying that you have to take the bad with the good. And of course growth is painful. Why, if you don't experience pain and struggle in your life, you don't learn anything. Everyone knows that!"

Everyone *believes* that, rather. Everyone, that is, who is still operating from the prevailing belief system that says it's a dog-eat-dog world, every man for himself, survival of the fittest. The aphorisms above are "logical" extensions of these beliefs in a hostile universe. And added to those is the idea arising out of the "clockwork universe" belief that we are each a very insignificant piece of machinery in that universe, and therefore we do not deserve very much. Happiness is undesirable not only because it keeps us from growing ("no pain, no gain") but also because we don't deserve it. We'd feel guilty if we had it. As if this weren't enough to defeat happiness as a goal, we also tend to associate happiness with drugs, sex, and even violence, all of which can be "dangerous." The hedonistic "Eat, drink, and be merry, for tomorrow we die," attitude does not appeal to a lot of us, not only because it seems to accomplish nothing but also because, as we may have learned from experience, it fails to be amusing for long. The Italian film *La Dolce Vita* portrayed "the sweet life" as quite the opposite, in which a group of people went to greater and greater extremes merely to avoid boredom for a few precious moments. They were the privileged, rich, and beautiful, with all the time and money in the world to have fun and to enjoy themselves, and yet they were miserable. The more they sought happiness the more it eluded them. Many people identified with this statement.

So, all in all, as a culture we tend not to believe in happiness, not even to have it as an ideal to reach for. Happiness, we believe, can be dangerous, and it is elusive; happiness is a block to growth, happiness is something we don't deserve. And so, distrusting happiness, we seek unhappiness instead, using it as a way of dealing with life.

In a marvelous book called *To Love Is to Be Happy With,* the author, Barry Kaufman, talks about how people teach themselves to believe in unhappiness.

> I dreaded obesity and rejection in order to motivate myself to diet. I feared lung cancer so that I could stop smoking. I became anxious about unemployment as a way of pushing myself to be more conscientious and to work harder. I felt guilty to punish myself now in order to prevent myself from repeating a "bad" behavior in the future. I became melancholy when someone I loved was unhappy in order to show them I cared. I got angry at those in my employ to make them move faster . . . I saw people punish in order to prevent, fear death in order to live, hate war in order to stay in touch with their desire for peace . . . I was taught that I "had to" be unhappy sometimes and that it was even "good" or productive to be unhappy . . . Unhappiness was the tattoo of a thinking, feeling man. It was the mark of sensitivity. It was also considered . . . to be the only "reasonable" and "human" response to a difficult and problematic society.

In other words, if you're happy you won't grow, you won't learn, you won't be motivated to do anything about your "problems," you won't get other people to do what you want, you won't care about others' suffering, you won't be sensitive, you won't be human. The term "idiot's delight" implies you have to be crazy to be happy about everything. No "reasonable" human being could be that way!

Kaufman uses what he calls the Option Process (which he says is a way of life more than anything else) in counseling, and it consists basically of asking yourself (or, as a counselor, others) three basic questions:

1. *What are you unhappy about?* What do you mean by that, or what about that makes you unhappy?
2. *Why are you unhappy about that?* What do you mean by that?
3. *Why do you believe that?* Or do you believe that? Or *what are you afraid would happen if you weren't unhappy about that?*

In using this line of questioning, Kaufman and his clients discovered that their being upset or angry or otherwise unhappy with a situation in their lives often had to do with the belief that they *should* be unhappy in order to show their caring, or that they *should* be unhappy in order to accomplish what they wanted to, or that they *should* be unhappy in order to prove they were human. But as they continued asking the same questions, they came to see that there really was no reason one had to be unhappy in order to deal with life. In fact, their unhappy feelings interfered with their ability to see the situation clearly and to make decisions. The following dialogue is quoted verbatim from Kaufman's book (pages 143–147) to show you how this line of questioning works and the insights it leads to.

Q. *What are you unhappy about?*
A. About what I did.

Q. What did you do?
A. When my husband Tom was away at a convention, Gary dropped by. He wasn't aware that Tom wouldn't be home. In fact, he had just come specifically to see him. You know how good friends don't have to make appointments. And then I was alone with nothing to do and he was really free for the evening, having planned to spend it with Tom and me. So . . . so, I suggested he stay. That seemed harmless enough. Maybe it was the drinks?

Q. The drinks?
A. Yes, I poured some sherry for both of us and one glass led to another. Then, I guess, it just happened. I mean it wasn't planned or anything. I'm not even sure I really wanted it. I just can't believe I would do that . . . it's just not me. I feel so cheap.

Q. What do you mean by "cheap"?
A. My husband is out breaking his neck while I'm home in bed with another man . . . and not just another man, a dear friend. Sounds like some silly daytime soap opera. [Crying] But it isn't you know; it's me.

Q. *What about that makes you so unhappy?*
A. That I slipped, that I was out of control.

Q. *Why is that so disturbing?*
A. I guess it shows me when I let loose, play it by ear, I'm really terrible. I'm not that classic dissatisfied woman looking to shack up. I really have a reasonably decent relationship with my husband . . . it's not perfect, but certainly not bad enough to warrant cheating behind his back. [Sobbing softly] I mean for just one lousy night over three months ago, all this . . . I've been paying ever since.

Q. What do you mean?

A. I mean I feel terrible, I can't stand myself. If I could only take it all back, I would.

Q. Why?
A. Because I shouldn't have done it. I didn't set out to cheat on my marriage and I certainly don't want my life filled with lies.

Q. I understand that's not what you are now wanting, but why do you feel bad about what you did three months ago?
A. Why do I feel bad about what I did? [Long pause] When you do something wrong you naturally feel bad.

Q. Possibly . . . but why do you *"naturally" feel bad?*
A. [Smiling] You know, I really don't know why. That sounds silly. I was going to say it's automatic, but that doesn't seem right. I guess feeling bad is another way to say I feel guilty.

Q. Okay, fine. If you define your feelings as guilty, why do you feel guilty?
A. Why? Wouldn't anyone feel just a bit guilty after cheating on their husband in his own bed with, no less, a family friend.

Q. Maybe, but each of us would have our own reasons for feeling guilty. What are yours?
A. Well, I guess I see it as betraying a trust. If Tom and I had decided to have an open marriage, with each of us going our own way from time to time, then it would be okay. It's the undercover part that I feel guilty about.

Q. What do you mean?
A. I think I'd feel better if he knew. It would be in the open. I guess, in a way, that's also what I'm most afraid will happen. I don't really know how he'd react . . . especially since the man was Gary. Damn, I don't know why I let myself get into this. I was so incredibly stupid. First, I blamed Gary; but he didn't drag me into the bedroom. We both went hand in hand. Two very consenting adults. Why the hell did I do it? I'm furious with myself.

Q. *Why are you angry with yourself?*
A. I shouldn't have done it; it says something about my character. I wouldn't want Tom doing the same thing. Everything is upside-down. Mostly, I'm unhappy and feeling so guilty that I ever did it in the first place.

Q. *What are you afraid would happen if you didn't feel guilty about having the affair?*

A. That I might do it again and again. [Startled expression] Wow, did I say that? I never realized I believed that before.

Q. Are you saying that by being guilty about having an affair, it will prevent you from entering into other ones?

A. *Yes, that's exactly what I mean. If I weren't remorseful about it, I might do it again . . . wouldn't I?*

Q. Well, maybe we can explore it. Do you want to have another affair?

A. No, really and truly no.

Q. *Do you believe if you were not unhappy or guilty that you would?*

A. As I think about it, it doesn't make any sense. Even if I don't feel guilty, I still know that I don't want to hop in bed with anyone other than Tom. That seems so clear now. I guess I was afraid that if I wasn't guilty, it meant I wanted to do it again. [Smiling] That's beautiful. I see why I've been feeling so guilty. But . . . but isn't it normal to feel bad when you've done something wrong?

Q. What do you think?

A. I don't know any more. I guess I'm believing if I don't feel guilty, maybe it means I'm callous . . . that I don't care.

Q. *Why do you believe that?*

A. Because . . . just maybe that's what I've been taught. If you do something wrong or bad, you're supposed to feel bad.

Q. Why?

A. I thought I answered that . . . you are supposed to.

Q. Sure, but why *are you supposed to feel bad when you do something "wrong?"*

A. I guess to punish yourself. Retribution. It's a crazy learning process that I've done for years.

Q. Do you need the punishment of feeling bad or unhappy in order to learn?

A. No. Of course not. I see that now. It's strange. I don't feel at all guilty right now and for the first time in three months, I'm absolutely clear. I don't want to go outside my marriage and I'm not afraid that I will. Before, I felt so guilty I couldn't even get to what I wanted. I just kept beating myself up.

Q. And now?

A. Well, I guess, whether I feel guilty or not, it doesn't change what
    I did. I guess hating myself was my way of making it all right.
    You know the old story . . . after you pay for your transgres-
    sions, everything is okay again.

Q. What do you want?
A. [Visibly drifting . . . after several minutes, no answer]

Q. What are you feeling?
A. You know what popped into my head. I thought I'd like to tell
    Tom everything, but for the life of me, I couldn't come up with
    a reason. I guess I also think if I tell him without being totally
    broken-up, tearful and frightened, he would think I was terrible.

Q. What are you saying?
A. That I'd like to tell him, but I'm afraid if I don't seem guilt-
    ridden and miserable, he wouldn't accept it. Look, I sure don't
    want to ruin my marriage over anything like this.

Q. Do you believe you would?
A. I wouldn't. [Smiling] In many ways this whole thing has just reaf-
    firmed what I want . . . which is my husband. I guess my mar-
    riage does have some real problems . . . especially
    communication problems. Maybe that's what this was all for . . .
    bringing things into the open. Without guilt, I even feel freer to
    really try to understand. I guess before I was too afraid.

Q. What do you want?
A. To feel good, which is exactly what I'm beginning to do right
    now for the first time in three months. It never occurred to me
    that I didn't have to feel guilty . . . that, in fact, I made myself
    guilty. Strange, how my response felt so automatic.

Q. And now?
A. I see how I used the guilt. I guess I can feel good about myself
    and be a loving, caring wife without punishing myself. Funny
    . . . now that I'm no longer unhappy about what I did, I'm much
    more willing to look at it.

Exercise

1. To give yourself practice in this line of questioning, I would like you to choose a past incident that you still feel unhappy about despite doing all of the exercises to this point, and to go through a dialogue similar to the one above, asking the three basic questions and answering them. If you can find a partner to do this exercise with, all the better. Continue the line of questioning until you feel a sense of relief, until you decide it is okay not to be unhappy about whatever it is.

2. Here are some aphorisms to replace the ones given on page 101. Read each one and if it sounds true to you, go on to the next one. If it gives you trouble, ask yourself why. What beliefs do you have standing in the way? What new beliefs could you develop instead?

> "Growth comes through happiness."
> "The less pain, the more gain."
> "Life is a joy."
> "Life is a rose garden."
> "You can have it ALL!"
> "No one, ever, has to justify his existence."
> "There is no such thing as bad."
> "Life just keeps getting better and better."
> "You don't have to pay for pleasure."
> "The rosier life is, the better."

Habit of Happiness #18

When you find yourself feeling unhappy about something, ask yourself what you are unhappy about, why that makes you unhappy, and what would happen if you weren't unhappy. Continue this line of questioning until you have convinced yourself that it is not necessary to be unhappy about the situation. Make happiness your choice!

19

Appreciation and Gratitude

Many years ago, my husband's brother and his wife came down to Hawaii from the East Coast to visit us. I had never met them before, and I was also eight months pregnant. However, because my husband was very busy at that time with his new business, I took it upon myself to show the couple around the island. Literally.

We drove down to Waikiki and past Kapiolani Park at its edge, and then took the road that goes around halfway up the slopes of Diamond Head Crater, stopping at the lighthouse lookout with its wide vista of curling waves and surfers and outrigger canoes. We then proceeded south to Kokohead Crater and to the arid volcanic part of the island where the cobalt sea crashes on the porous black lava, and where the "blowhole" spumes spray fifty feet into the air. We rounded the southern end of the island and started north on the eastern, windward side where the wind-eroded, corrugated cliffs tower close to the powdery white beaches. The sea is turquoise along here, and rough, flashing with white caps.

We continued on up the coast past Kaneohe Bay, past the ancient Hawaiian fishing grounds, and Chinaman's Hat (a small island offshore that looks just like its name), through the tiny picturesque towns of Ka'a'awa and Hauula, past the Polynesian Cultural Center at Laie, and reached the northern end of the island at Kahuku. Here we headed west, passing cane fields to the left, and to the right the many surfing beaches of poster fame. It was January, and the waves were at twelve to fifteen feet. Reaching the arty village of Haleiwa, we headed south once more, climbing up onto the rolling plains where pineapple fields abound and two mountain ranges line the horizon to the right and left, and then descended to Honolulu, going through Chinatown—the harbor, with its huge freighters, a few blocks to the right—and then past Ala Moana Park. We returned to our house, which was nestled on the slopes of verdant Mount Tantalus in the Manoa section of town, where the university is located.

We had left about noon, and it was almost six when we got back. My husband was home from work. The first question he asked his brother was, "Well, what do you think of Oahu?"

Jake paused a moment, as if surprised by the obvious question. "Oh, yeah, well, it was . . . uh . . . different. Uhh . . . I thought the waves would be bigger."

I wasn't surprised at Jake's answer, because for the entire drive he and his wife, Dotsy, had been wrangling with one another. This did not seem to be unusual (as the days ahead would show) but rather their accustomed way of interacting. They were constantly nagging one another about something. "Did you bring the camera?" "No, did you?" "I thought *you* had it!" "I told *you* to bring it!" and so on. We stopped four times along the way to get cold drinks and fast food, for they were hungry and thirsty and hot. When we would be driving past a scene I particularly loved, I would say something like "Look at that red earth there with the fuchsia bougainvillea against it. Isn't that gorgeous?" and they might (or might not) interrupt their argument long enough to turn their heads and look in the direction I was pointing. Usually they wouldn't say anything in reply, and they'd quickly resume where they left off without missing a beat. The scenery barely registered on them, and certainly my generosity in showing them around went unnoticed.

A friend of mine recently wrote about the cottage she bought on an island off the coast of Maine. This has been a lifelong dream of hers, and she *loves* it there. The pictures she sent me are fantastic. Last Thanksgiving, she and a man she'd met who also has a house there decided to have their dinner at her cottage on the island, and the two of them together took the four-hour drive and one-hour ferry ride to get there from Boston. A couple of hours later they went to the tiny airstrip on the island to pick up three of the man's friends from New York, who emerged from the small plane "dripping in black leather and high-heeled plastic-soled boots, and made up like you wouldn't believe." The first thing they wanted to know was where the bars were. "There aren't any." "None? No bars?" "Nope. None." By now it was about sunset, and they all drove to a point where they could see the sun set over the bay; the New Yorkers were "screaming obscenities at each other because of their slick boots, which didn't climb so well." Later on in the evening, they wondered where they could get "the paper." Well, the *New York Times* came to that island only on Sunday. This was the last straw. The city slickers were totally bummed out.

This is a chapter on appreciation and gratitude, and, of course, my two examples illustrate the opposite. I am sure all of you have had similar experiences, and I rather imagine that as far as you're concerned if you never see those people again (unappreciative ingrates that they are) it would be too soon. If for no other reason than friendship, then, showing appreciation and gratitude is a good habit to get into. Have you noticed that, when someone expresses his or her appreciation to you, or thanks you for some effort you have made, you feel like doing *more* for that person? It isn't at all the same thing if that person merely *feels* appreciation or gratitude, although that is a lot better than *not* having those feelings, but the *expression* of that appreciation and gratitude is magical in its effect not only on the receiver, but also on the giver.

It feels *great* to express appreciation and thanks, and it feels *great* to receive it. You just want to give that person more and more! (That is, if the appreciation and gratitude are *heartfelt*. As we saw in chapter 15, if your sole motive in expressing appreciation and gratitude is simply to win that person's approval and/or to ensure his or her friendship, no amount of approval and acceptance will feel good to you, because you don't believe you are worthy yourself and because you know you're being a phony by seeking approval in that fashion.)

There is a lot more to appreciation and gratitude, though, than noticing what people are doing for you or responding enthusiastically to what they say. You don't need other people in order to feel (and express) appreciation and gratitude. All you "need" is yourself. Remember, if you find that a lot of people in your life do things for you that you appreciate and feel like giving a heartfelt thanks for, *you* created that reality for yourself. You not only owe these people appreciation and thanks but also, more basically, owe yourself appreciation and thanks for having created this reality for yourself.

And, since you are always with yourself, and not always with other people, a lot more opportunities exist to appreciate and thank yourself than others. Since it feels so good and makes the receiver desirous of giving more and more, why not give yourself this appreciation and gratitude?

As we've already seen in chapter 3, it feels good to pat ourselves on the back for all of the beautiful things we have created for ourselves. Giving thanks goes a step further. If you get into the habit of giving thanks to yourself you will find that this practice not only feels good and enhances your relationships with others (for you will find yourself thanking them more, too) but also brings more and more of what you have expressed your appreciation for to yourself. A snowball effect!

Exercise

1. Look out of your window. What you see out there is what you created. Appreciate this and thank it for being there. Thank yourself for manifesting it.
2. Look around your living room. You have created all of this. Appreciate each item and thank it. Thank yourself.
3. During your next meal, take time to appreciate the food and thank it. Thank yourself for bringing it to you in space-time.
4. Notice all the things you do for yourself—the ideas that come to you, the tasks you do for yourself so faithfully, the leisure-time activities you enjoy. Appreciate these things and thank yourself for doing them for you.

Habit of Happiness #19

Every day, take ten minutes to write a thank-you note to your-self for all the beautiful things you have created for yourself in the past twenty-four hours: the sun in the trees, the cat purring in your lap, the smile of a child, the joke someone made at work, the insight you had, the letter from a friend. Revel in how good it feels to do this, and savor the appreciation and gratitude you are giving to yourself. Notice how much more you want to do for yourself.

20

Everything *Really Does* Happen for the Best

One of the many advantages of getting older is the perspective it gives you. When I was younger—really until my late thirties—I could see very little pattern to my life, other than the everyday routine: Get up, get dressed, eat, prepare for classes, go to the university, take classes, talk with fellow students, come home, swim, cook dinner, entertain self and/or others, go to bed. It's true, I could look back on my childhood and see some patterns in it that I was repeating now, such as moving around a lot. When I was a kid we had moved from one house (and sometimes one city or state) to another every year or two. And I had continued doing this after I left my parents' home. But there were many aspects of my life that seemed to be so random. One thing I did know: The living pattern of "the average middle-class American" (whoever that might be!) did not attract me. I saw that living pattern as follows: getting married, settling down in the suburbs, having three kids, two cars, and a dog, the wife staying home, the husband working forty hours a week in an upwardly mobile white-collar job, barbecuing in the backyard, two-week summer vacations on a camping trip, helping the kids with their homework, driving them to all of their many extracurricular activities, saving money for a college fund, getting the children married off, taking care of grandchildren.

But though I found this pattern unappealing (for years it was downright depressing to me to contemplate: I think I must have feared it would be my lot despite all evidence/actions to the contrary, and at the same time I must have envied people who knew what they wanted to do with their lives), still it *was* a pattern and in that there was security. Or so it seemed to me, who saw little pattern to my own existence. I would have liked a few more *predictables* in my life other than the sun rising and setting. I would have liked to know where I was going and why.

For instance, why, really, had I chosen to go to graduate school in my thirties, with a husband and small child and plenty to do around the house? I hadn't planned on grad school, and I didn't have any particular thirst for more knowledge, or, rather, I didn't have any particular area of study in mind. There was much I wanted to know, but I couldn't boil it down to specific subject matter. Certainly, any money I might make resulting from my higher education was not needed. It had seemed a whimsical (if not utterly frivolous) choice at the time: A friend of my husband who was heading up a new program at the university suggested I apply to it, as they needed students, and they had cushy grants going begging. So, I got into that particular master's degree program because: A friend suggested it, I could get my tuition and even some living expenses paid for while doing it, and it was something different to do. I did *not* choose the program because I had any recognizable interest in the courses offered.

As I see it now, though, the choice to go to graduate school was one of the most important decisions I ever made in terms of the living patterns it made possible and the lessons/learning it set up, and which I carried through on. First of all, once I found out what linguistics was all about, I was fascinated with the subject, and I couldn't do enough studying. The research I did at that time set up a lifelong pattern of careful reading and note taking, which stands me in good stead to this day. Then, because I was such a good student, I was offered a job at the same university even before I got my degree. Just as they had once needed students in the program, they now needed instructors, and even though I was just barely ahead of the new students, they felt they could use me. This part-time job turned into a full-time position and led to tenure and promotion first to an assistant professorship and then to an associate professorship. (Today it is impossible to get tenure in that department without a Ph.D.)

This university teaching job was another long-term pattern in my life, and during those times when all other aspects of my life seemed chaotic, it served as my security blanket. Whatever else, I always had this absorbing job and working conditions that offered a lot of freedom, both in and out of the classroom. I particularly enjoyed the long summer vacations (even when I spent most of the time researching and writing in my field), and I *loved* the sabbaticals that were mandatory after every six years of teaching. To get a year off at half-pay in order to refresh my mind—well, that just felt so luxurious to me! If I hadn't had these sabbaticals I would not have done my extensive traveling, which is another pattern, related to but different from my earlier pattern of moving from one place to another. The two patterns have come together, actually, with moving and traveling being different aspects of the same thing.

Another very important pattern that my decision to go to graduate school led to was my writing. Actually, that pattern started when I was eight years old and decided to write a novel. I even outlined six or eight chapters and wrote part of the first one. I also started keeping a journal, which has continued intermittently over the years. But the writing I got into at the university was of a different kind. It arose out of a strongly felt need, so far as I was concerned, for decent teaching materials for writing students.

When I first started teaching, there were no appropriate textbooks in existence for my students, who were mature and intelligent and spoke Japanese or Korean or Cantonese or Tagalog (to name just a few) as a first language. The usual books for such students were insultingly simplistic. So, I began developing teaching materials to use in the classroom (and also wrote articles for the professional journals explaining my theory and method) and ended up getting two books for writing students published before I left the university two years ago. Had I not had all of those years of experience in writing teaching materials I'm not sure I would have been ready to attempt writing *Create Your Own Reality,* which then would have meant that *this* book would still have been a vague desire in the back of my mind.

When I look back on that Nancy of twenty-six years ago, not knowing what she was doing or why, deciding to follow an impulse (which seemed suspect to her), I feel such an appreciation for her for all she did for me, the Nancy of today, that I cannot thank her enough.

For that matter I cannot thank enough the Nancy who decided to divorce her husband and even to leave her kids—one of them then only two—with him for a time (both of those decisions were made amid much doubt and guilt) for what she has done for me, and the learning/lessons she set up that I have followed through on. What gifts she has given me! What gifts all of my past selves have given me!

A very dear friend of mine, Jenny, called me recently to say that she had been to visit her grandmother, who is old and sickly, and then her father, who has chronic emphysema.

"Nancy," she said. "I have just been given two wonderful gifts."

"What are they?" I asked.

"Well," she replied, "I had assumed that both my grandmother and my father were going to leave me all their money since I am the only heir of this generation."

"Yes, I remember you telling me that."

"Just to make sure, I brought it up with them, and they told me they had no such plans."

"Really?"

"Yes, and I am so glad, because I realize I had been *counting* on this money coming in the not-too-distant future. This meant I didn't have to really get serious about supporting myself because I would soon be 'saved.' "

I was so glad Jenny had this insight. She had earlier told me that the most important challenge in her life at that time was "getting her money trip together." For years she had dabbled with this and that but had never taken supporting herself seriously. Whenever she needed money she had relied on the support of men she was involved with, or friends, or family. And she owed the government fifteen thousand dollars in back taxes for a failed business venture she had gone into with a male partner who had put up all the money. Because she had never solved the money problem it kept coming back to haunt her, of course, and she had finally decided it was time to do something about it. And, in a small way, she had begun to do just that.

Then along came the revelation that she really could not expect anyone "out there" to solve the problem for her: She was not going to inherit. It seems that this bit of information came at just the right time for her. Earlier she would not have understood its implications, and it may have seemed like a cruel blow. But now, after focusing in on the challenge ahead of her and having this one last obstacle to her carrying it out removed—an obstacle in the form of "salvation"—she is now free to go ahead and do what she had to do for herself.

The point is that what might appear scary or disappointing or burdensome to us at a particular point in time is happening for a purpose from a larger perspective, and that purpose always is to help us to grow and to learn. From that larger perspective (which may scan years, decades, generations, or even lifetimes) there is no such thing as good or bad, right or wrong, better or worse. There is only growth and learning and expansion of consciousness. From that perspective there are no problems, only challenges.

A belief a lot of us operate under is that we learn through trial and error, through our failures as well as our successes. And, actually, that belief can be a positive one, especially for people who are coming off the belief that it is not okay to make a mistake. To believe that you can learn through your mistakes is a much more positive way to look at things than to believe you are bad when you err. My goal in this chapter, though, has been to show you that there are no such things as errors or mistakes or failures from a wider perspective of yourself and your life, only lessons learned along the path of becoming. Having the belief that there are no errors, mistakes, or failures is an even more positive way to look at life, resulting in even more positive feelings about yourself. What I am hoping to do is to give you an ever-wider perspective on yourself as creator and actor in the play that is your life, knowing that the more we see and the more we know, the more confident we become. And the more confident we become, the happier we are.

Exercise

1. There is much to be learned through *not* having what we want. For example, Jenny was learning about money—her attitudes toward and resistance to it—through the lack of money. Think of something in your life that you want to have but do not have—it could take a material form like money, or it could be a relationship, a skill, or a perspective. Think of what you are learning through not having this thing. You could be learning that you don't really want it after all, or you could be learning that you are afraid of having it or that you don't feel deserving, skilled, or experienced enough. It might help to look at times in the past when you wanted something but didn't get it and to see what you learned from those experiences. From a wider perspective you may be able to see the learning behind what you presently lack. In any case, see if you can pinpoint what you have learned so far and what more you need to learn, either to have what you want or to let go of wanting it.

2. Think of some "problems" you had in your past that you no longer have today. From your present perspective can you see that they were not problems at all but challenges? That they were gifts to you from yourself, to give yourself the opportunity to learn and to grow in that area?

3. Imagine yourself as the you of five years from now. From that perspective view your current challenges and see how necessary they are in order for the current you to be who you are. See what having those challenges has done for you and what you learned from them. Thank that self who learned those lessons in order for you to be who you are.

4. As we saw in chapter 18, the prevailing belief system dictates that growth comes through pain and struggle. And, true to form, we see a lot of pain and struggle in the world-at-large. What is the world-at-large learning from this pain and struggle? View not only your own life but that of the masses as being a series of challenges, as lessons from which to grow and to learn. What lessons has the world learned in the past? What is it learning now? If you take this perspective, there is much to be optimistic about.

Habit of Happiness #20

Whenever you find yourself viewing something in your life in a negative light, change that negative to a positive by seeing whatever it is as a challenge, as a gift from yourself, as a lesson from which to learn and to grow. Get in the habit of viewing your life from a larger perspective than the usual day-to-day one, and notice what you have learned from your challenges. Have faith that everything happens for the best, not only for yourself but also for the world-at-large.

21

You *Are* Your Soul

The prevailing belief system, the one that holds the scientific method and logical empiricism in high esteem, does not "officially" recognize the existence of soul. Since what is generally understood to be soul is not material, it cannot be empirically validated the argument goes. Its existence therefore can never be proven one way or another, and so there is no point in wasting one's time on it.

Nevertheless, the concept of soul is very much alive and well. We do not have to be religious or even call ourselves "spiritually oriented" to believe that there is something *more* to reality than what we see "out there" or, for that matter, what we normally see "within." Most of the metaphysical literature I've read talks of "higher" sources of knowledge, of "divine guidance," of spirit guides, or something of that sort. In every case the soul concept is linked to God or "the Force" or "All That Is" or "the Powers That Be." Whatever it is, it connects us to the unseen, inner world.

The trouble with most of these ideas of soul is that they imply a separation between "us" and "it." Even the literature that says the soul is *part* of us implies that this part is elusive, difficult to get in touch with, something quite apart from our "ordinary" mind, something beyond our conscious awareness, something ineffable, ultimately mysterious. And for this reason we can never be sure whether "we" are really in touch with "it" or not. We tend not to think that our everyday selves have much to do with the "other" "more spiritual," and therefore "better" self. We tend to see our everyday selves who partake of material reality as inferior, less wise, less evolved, and less spiritual than what we perceive of as soul—which gives us just one more reason not to appreciate who we are.

And yet, as Seth has said so beautifully, "The body is the soul in flesh." Throughout his books he says that there are no separations to the self, that "we" are the soul's expression of itself in three-dimensional reality. He does say that it is sometimes convenient for the sake of discussion to distinguish the inner self, who is the information-processor and manifestor, from the ego or outer self, who is the believer and the experiencer in space-time reality. But in actuality, they are one and the same, a unified whole, a gestalt of conscious energy. Body, mind, and soul—three ways of "looking at" the same thing. "We"—the ego or outer self—*are* the soul or inner self in space-time.

But because we have come to think of the soul as separate from and higher than we are, we don't even recognize it in our day-to-day lives. We don't realize how *familiar* it is, what an intimate part of us it really is. And I think it is because of this sense of separation—coupled with the ever-growing interest in the spiritual side of life, which is a reflection of the emerging belief system—that so many "channels" have been appearing on the scene. People still don't quite trust their own inner wisdom, and so they project it "out there" so that they can believe in its authority. A lot of mediums—Jane Roberts for instance—go into deep trances and do not directly hear what their channeled entity says. Others are aware of it happening at the time. In every case, though, the mediums regard the entity channeled as separate from themselves, in touch with higher knowledge that "they" could not possibly have come in contact with by "themselves."

I may be in for a lot of argument from those of you who believe, as Jane Roberts believed, that Seth was a distinct and separate personality from her (or that Ramtha is separate from J. Z. Knight, and so on, with all the well-known mediums), and until now (just as I was writing this, as a matter of fact—this was not "planned") my stance was that the distinction did not really matter. What was important was the validity and usefulness of the information in my own life. And, because I continue to find Seth's material the most meaningful of all the material I have delved into (and it is a lot), I have pretty much stuck with his teachings over the years.

But in thinking it over while writing this book, I have come to the conclusion that the distinction (between the idea that the entities are separate beings from the self who channels them and the idea that they are a part of that self) is worth making for an important reason: So long as we regard channeled entities as something apart from the channelers, it limits our potential. It limits to some extent the potential of the channelers themselves when they believe that it is not "they" who have this wisdom but some entity they are tuning into, and it limits to a greater extent the potential of those who listen to the channeler giving out the information. The channelers give credit for the information to their "spirit guide" or whoever ("I must ask my spirit guide for the answer") rather than own the power and skill they are displaying. And the people in the audience not only credit the information as coming from some "higher" source but also believe that they are not themselves capable of getting in touch with that outside source except through others.

And this is despite what many great teachers have said: "Trust thyself," "The answer lies within," and "Thou art God." Those of us who have done reading in metaphysics or religion have come across such sayings countless times, and yet, for the most part, we still tend to treat metaphysical information as coming from some "higher" authority. I think this is a holdover from the old (still prevalent) belief system, with its idea that the limits of man's knowledge extend to the limits of time and space, and therefore any information that we get from beyond these dimensions must come from some source "outside." Another old belief operating here is one in competition and "better than/worse than," which leads to the belief that there are some people out there—authorities—who can tell us what to do better than we can tell ourselves. If we truly believed in the universe as an "interconnected web of events," as a hologram with "the world in every grain of sand," then we would know that we can get in touch with anything we want to know. All of us can develop the ability to tap full knowledge of the universe.

This does not mean, of course, that we cannot learn a great deal from others—whether those others are people "like us" or "higher" sources of knowledge as Seth is reputed to be. The point is we could learn even more if we believed in our own limitless potential for knowledge and *also*—this is important—realized that each of us is unique and thus has his or her own unique perspective on the information from the limitless pool available to all of us. We interpret the information according to that perspective: The "same" information coming from you is different from that coming from me. Also, whatever information we get from someone else, we interpret and use in our own unique way. You interpret and use the Seth information differently from the way I do. This book is not intended as "the only true gospel" but as an example of how the Seth material is interpreted and used by one person, in order, I hope, to inspire you to try your own interpretation and use.

What I'm saying, then, is that I see some benefit in believing that each of us—the "us" we know as "us"—has the power to access whatever information he or she seeks, for this not only empowers us to develop the ability to do so but also prevents us from giving away our power to the authorities "out there" (or "up there"). And, finally, it would benefit everyone if *everyone* got in touch with his or her own source of knowledge within, which is an intimate part of each person, for then we would all have everyone's perspective on the information. We would then come to really see and to really know that there is no authority for us except ourselves. We would trust our "everyday" selves totally.

But, you ask, how do we *do* this? Well, I have no easy answers. I do know that the better I get to know myself the more trusting I become in making choices, in following whims, in putting down these words on paper. A few years back I would never have said what I've said in this chapter without quoting some "outside authority" to give me "support." Today I am telling you, "This is what I think." Take it for what it's worth to you, and trust your particular interpretation of it. This process has worked for me; perhaps something similar will work for you, too.

Another thing I have come to know and to recognize is when my "soul" is talking to me. I know that voice within—and a very familiar one it is—which comes from what I know to be my soul (or inner self or creator self—choose the term that feels best to you.) This voice is different from that coming from what I have chosen to call in this book my "subpersonalities" in that *it never judges!* It is a gentle, joyful voice saying *"Isn't this fun? Wouldn't you just love to do that? Why don't you do this?"* It never tells me "I" am wrong in doing anything, or even that I *should* do something in the future. It is a voice I hear most often when I am by myself and relaxed or after a time when I have actively been seeking solutions in my life, after I have exhausted my "usual" sources of knowledge based on my experience so far in this space-time lifetime.

And it isn't only or even primarily by voice that I know my soul. I see its "hand" in my reality every day, via an "unexpected" phone call that gives me the information needed to decide on something, via a "feeling" that I want to do this or that, via the "coincidence" of meeting someone who "just happens" to have similar interests to mine, via "insights" I get about my own behavior or that of others, via spontaneous urges, and even via the gift of having something *not* happen that I thought I wanted to happen, only to find out later that I am much better off that it didn't.

I have found that the more I have consciously acknowledged and thanked this part of me, the more "visible" it has become, as if this wise but very permissive, accepting part of me has been waiting for "me" to be ready to accept its suggestions. Lately, the happiness I feel as my reality-creating becomes ever more to my liking, has a depth and resonance to it like a deep chord from the heart of my being: My soul sings.

Exercise

1. This week make a point of listening to the voice of your soul, of that creative, joyful inner being. Spend some relaxed time alone, listening. It will be a soft, unobtrusive voice, and it will be positive, encouraging, and nonjudgmental. Every time you hear this voice, say hello to it and thank it. Ask it to be with you more.
2. Also this week, notice all the events, however unimportant, in which you sense clues coming from your soul, from your inner creator self. Try to see beyond coincidences, unexpected events, spontaneous urges, and the like to what these are clues to—what kind of a reality they are gently nudging you toward. Thank your soul and let it know you trust it.

Habit of Happiness #21

Listen to the voice of your soul and recognize how familiar it is, what an intimate part of your life it is. Acknowledge and thank it for all the suggestions and help it gives you in creating your reality.

22

On Reality-Creating

The reason I ended up writing my own teaching materials to use in my writing classes was that all of the textbooks I came across focused on the *product* of writing. A typical text would often begin by having the students look at passages of writing by professionals, which exemplified various means of developing ideas. They would then focus in on smaller bits of writing, exemplifying paragraph development, and then focus in on sentence construction. Spelling and punctuation and other "mechanics" of writing would usually be at the end. I considered it a boon if there was a section of the book devoted to getting ideas, or "invention" as it was sometimes called, for it seemed to me that this was a crucial skill to learn. But I could never figure out how to integrate such a skill with the product-oriented lessons of these typical texts, for from what I could see the generation of ideas was hampered by the requirement that the students write, say, a paragraph demonstrating a given means of development, such as chronological, cause-effect, or comparison and contrast.

I found that my students, faced with a preconceived mold within which to insert ideas, resorted to the most obvious and banal of ideas without exception. Since their task was, as they saw it, to come up with a "correct" form, why should they care about what ideas that form contained? And I couldn't blame them for this attitude, for when I had tried to do the same exercises I found myself doing the same thing. Whatever good ideas I might have had usually wouldn't fit into the mold, even if the mold had worked for another writer. It was frustrating to see all of these samples of great writing displayed in the textbooks and to find that, upon trying to emulate them, I turned out to be a mediocre product at best. If I, an experienced, published writer, turned out inferior writing under those restrictions, how could I expect my students to express themselves well in that way?

Many years would pass, though, before I came up with a workable solution to this dilemma and ended up writing a process-oriented workbook for writing students. I was helped by the research on the writing process that began in the seventies as other frustrated teachers like me cast about for a better approach than the old product-oriented one. The research showed that every person had his or her own strategies for writing; that writing was not a linear, word-by-word, paragraph-by-paragraph process, but a recursive one in which the writer was constantly looking back at what he had already said before going on, sometimes scanning several pages; that the more effective writers paid little attention to sentence structure or spelling, kept in mind the ideas they wanted to get down, and often had a plan of development (though rarely was this a "purely" chronological, or cause-effect, or comparison and contrast, or "textbook" type of development but an intermingling of all of those logical gambits depending on what the writer had to say); that the more skilled writers were more aware of their audiences than the unskilled writers, using a different vocabulary and even overall strategy depending on who they were writing for.

There were a lot of other findings, and all of them pointed to the conclusion that it does not work to try to teach students to write by showing them finished products and asking them to emulate those products. In fact, quite the opposite was true: All of the writers—skilled and unskilled—were able to write much better when they focused on the process of writing rather than on the product, when they focused on how to get their ideas (not yet in words) across rather than on a given structure within which to fit their ideas. They also learned a lot more about writing when they were allowed to create their own forms for their own ideas rather than when they were required to use a given idea and a given form. And, finally, they *liked* writing better when allowed to be creative with it.

I want to illustrate the difference in effect of these two approaches with a couple of examples. First there's Joanne, who takes the traditional English class. Her teacher assigns her a five-hundred-word theme on "happiness." The teacher tells the students what a theme is and gives them step-by-step instructions on how to write it. Begin by making an outline, composed of a thesis statement, followed by the topic sentences heading the paragraphs that support the thesis, and then come to a conclusion. (Some teachers think they are teaching the writing *process* in giving such instructions; what they are actually presenting is a *finished product.*)

Well, Joanne goes away from class with one main concern: those five hundred words. How is she ever going to think of that much to say about happiness? Now, sadness would be a different matter. She'd had a lot of experience with *that* lately, though she doubts she could write about it in the format the teacher has specified. She doesn't want to think about the assignment at all, so she doesn't—until one hour before the next class. She goes to the cafeteria for a cup of coffee, sits at a table by herself, writes her outline (which must be handed in with the composition), and then doggedly copies the sentences from it onto theme paper, adding a few details.

She counts her words: 483. What to do? She has to add more. No sweat. Adjectives and adverbs, she has found, are useful for padding, so she adds some: very, too, nice, interesting, sometimes, kind of, really, usually, many, few, much, sort of, so. She counts her words again: 502. Finished! She reads the composition to herself and feels embarrassed. It's so trite and awkward, certainly not her. But she has fulfilled the assignment. What a relief to have it done—it was so hard to make herself do it, and she can't see what she has learned from it all. She just hopes she gets a passing grade. She sure would hate to have to repeat this course. It's awful!

Down the hall from Joanne's English class is another one, and here the teacher tells the students he wants them to get across in words some strong feelings they have experienced. He says he does not want a description of the feeling but an *experience* of it. "Make us all feel as you did." He says he doesn't care whether it's a poem or a short story or an essay or a journal entry or a play or a newspaper article or a combination of all of them or something else. "Let the form follow from your discoveries as you write." A student asks him how many words it should be. "Enough to get you from the beginning to the end. And, no, I'm not going to show you what other people have done with this assignment. I want this to be strictly your own creation."

Jonathan doesn't know what to think of this teacher who doesn't seem to have any rules or guidelines, and it seems like a tough assignment. He begins by thinking about times in his life when he's had strong feelings, and finally he settles on the happiest moment in his life: falling in love. That's such a trite subject, he thinks, but it didn't seem trite to me experiencing it. How can I get it across so that it doesn't come off sounding trite? He writes down a description of the circumstances that led up to his falling in love, but when it comes to describing the feeling itself, it doesn't come off right at all. It's really corny. Then he thinks, it isn't the story itself that is important but the feeling. He visualizes himself four years ago, newly in love. He vividly recalls the moment of discovery and he relives it, bringing it into the present. He's exhilarated! In this happy mood he sits down at the type-writer and finds himself writing a funny, happy song. He can even hear the melody—it "just came" to him as he was writing. He decides he will write down the music as well as the words, and he gets out his guitar and figures out the chords. Then more words come to him, and he writes them down. At first he tries to make rhymes, but he cannot convey the spontaneous, joyful feeling and rhyme the words at the same time, so he goes for the feeling.

He gets so absorbed in what he is doing that he loses all track of time and is surprised to find, when he has gone over his song several times, changing words and phrases here and there, rearranging stanzas, and coming up with a terrific chorus, that it is 3:00 A.M. But he is not tired at all and feels really pleased with himself. Here he thought he was just writing something for an English assignment, and he ends up doing something he had always wanted to do but hadn't thought he had the talent for: writing the music and lyrics for a song.

He hopes he gets a good grade for this assignment, but it doesn't really matter because he enjoyed doing it and feels he learned a lot from it. Not only about writing songs but also about feeling happy. He realized he can bring happiness to himself at will through recalling that happy time four years ago. He thinks he may have heard some wise person or other say something like that before, but it hadn't meant anything to him at the time because he hadn't had the experience; he hadn't made the discovery for himself. In this philosophical mood he goes to bed. His last thought before sleep is "writing isn't that hard after all. Really, it's kind of fun!"

In Joanne's case, we saw that a focus on the product didn't feel good, while in Jonathan's case we saw that a focus on the process did. And the reason is that Joanne was oriented toward the future and out of touch with her own creativity. (The teacher saw to that!) On the other hand, Jonathan was right there in the present, where reality is created, and very much in touch with and in charge of his creativity. Both of them learned from the experience. Joanne learned how bad it feels to be stymied; Jonathan learned how good it feels to be freely creative. Joanne didn't think she had learned anything because the learning that took place was negative: what *not* to do. Thus she decided she hated writing. Jonathan, in contrast, did feel he had learned something: much more than he would have envisioned had he been focused on the product. Thus, he decided he liked writing.

Of course, all of this applies to any form of creativity, whether it be a piece of writing, a painting, a romance, a job, or a personality trait. Creativity and learning take place *now*—not at the end of a process. If you want to get the most out of that process, if you want to learn as fast and as happily as you can, focus in on the present and let the future take care of itself.

Let's take the case of people who decide to create the reality of having a million dollars. That particular product is what they want. Well, they are going to learn a lot about what *not* to do in the process of acquiring that million dollars. It is true, they may eventually get the money, but I'd be willing to bet that when they do they're not going to feel satisfied with themselves or it. For it wasn't really the product that was important but the *creative learning process*. Usually when a person wants a million dollars, the million dollars is only a *symbol* of what he really wants, and the essence behind that symbol is happiness—or fulfillment, or peace of mind, or something else—which can come in many different forms. To make a million dollars your goal is to limit yourself to but one of the many forms available and also, again, to orient yourself to the future and thus miss out on what you are learning right now. Let's put it this way: If you want happiness, there's no way you can learn to be happy without experiencing happiness. You can't read about how to be happy and expect to wake up some time in the future and find yourself happy. You learn to be happy by *being happy!*

We create in order to learn and to grow. It is the learning and the growing that is important, not whatever forms (products) our creations take. And, to the extent that we are consciously aware of the learning and growing behind our creations, we will impede or enhance our progress. To focus single-mindedly on a million dollars, waiting for it to manifest before permitting ourselves to feel happy and fulfilled, is to miss out on what is happening *now* as we progress toward that goal. If we instead realized that a million dollars was symbolic of success, or security, or emotional richness, or whatever, and were open to whatever "reality" came along that gave us the feeling of success, or security, or emotional richness, we would come to see that we already have what we want every moment of our lives: Our reality reflects back to us the essence we are focused on. Being there is the process of getting there!

Being successful or secure or emotionally rich is a continually changing process, not a finished product. Unlike writing, which does end up eventually in a fixed, static form (a book, an article, etc.), the process of reality-creating never ends—there is no product, no final form. When my writing students were helped to become aware of what they were doing as they created the written product, their written product improved. When you become aware of what you are doing as you see the products of your creation constantly shifting before you, you become much more skilled at creating what you really want, moving from one learning to the next, instead of repeating the same lessons over and over, still trying to get that million dollars.

The imagination plays a crucial role in reality-creating, for it is a testing ground. Research has shown that the nervous system cannot tell the difference between an imagined experience and a "real" one. What you experience in your imagination is just as "real" as what you experience in space-time. That is why people have learned to play golf through imagining themselves playing it, imagining themselves holding the club in a certain way, feeling themselves take a swing, hearing the club hit the ball, seeing the ball fly through the air. Mental practicing brings the same results as physical practicing! Through consciously using your imagination, envisioning yourself in the process of becoming successful, or secure, or emotionally rich, or whatever it is that is the essence of the symbols you want to manifest, you give yourself practice and thus skill in creating the reality you want for yourself. In your imagination you can try out different symbols to see how they feel and select those that feel the best. This saves "time" in the "real" world.

The same is true of dreams. In our dreams, we hypothesize and test out possible realities for ourselves. The more you can get in touch with your dreaming process, the more you can be consciously aware of how you create your reality—the process behind the product. I have not dealt with dreams in this book not because I don't think they're important, but because so many good books have been written on dreaming: It is a very powerful process, as many writers have realized. Suffice it to say that remembering and writing down your dreams and learning to recognize what particular symbols you use in the process will help you to understand why you create the reality that you do, and can lead to some very creative dreaming indeed!

To sum up, the more you concentrate on process rather than product, the more quickly you will learn what you have decided to learn. And the better you know the essence behind the form, the better you will be at consciously manifesting what your heart truly desires.

Exercise

1. Look at the material objects you have acquired and try to determine what they symbolize to you; what the essence is behind the form. That essence might be pride, success, happiness, richness, harmony, peace—the list could go on and on. Realize that the same objects may very well represent something entirely different to other people. Find your own personal symbols for those objects. Then, in your imagination, envision having even more of that essence; realize that it can come to you in many forms you may not have thought of.

2. Ask yourself what you absolutely love to do. Your loving to do it is indication that you have achieved essence in that way. What is that essence? Envision having even more of it in ever more forms.

3. Ask yourself what you are committed to. What is the essence of those commitments? Imagine yourself achieving that essence, feel what it is like to experience that essence.

4. Notice when you are thinking in a product-oriented way. For instance, if you say, "I am a loving person," you are thinking of yourself as a static, finished product. (Also you are putting a judgment on yourself and others: "They are not as loving as/more loving than I am.") Change that statement to "What is the most loving thing I can do with my life?"

5. Look at your doubts about yourself. They reflect beliefs that stand in the way of reality-creating. Write down all of the reasons you believe you cannot have what you want—get these beliefs out in the open where you can deal with them. Substitute a positive belief for each negative belief. For instance, you might say that you cannot have a lot of money because you aren't good at earning it (that is, you believe that you haven't been good at it *in the past*). Change this belief to "I am learning what's involved in making lots of money." Make sure that the belief you substitute sounds reasonable to you, that it seems entirely possible to achieve.

Habit of Happiness #22

Get in the habit of looking beyond your space-time reality to the essence on which it is based. And, in your imagination, always focus on the process of becoming, not on the product.

23

Creating World Peace

By this time, I hope you have come firmly to believe and feel that you create your own reality, that you are entirely responsible for the reality you create. I hope that you have found some tools that will help you in creating the best possible reality for yourself. I hope that you have developed the skill of being happy through habitually believing in things that reflect back your happiness. If you have, there is really no need for this chapter. You are already doing your share in creating world peace through being peaceful yourself.

However, I have found that a lot of people do not really believe that it is enough "just" to be peaceful, "just" to live a peaceful life. They feel that they must "do something" in order to promote world peace. And if that is their belief, then they will not be entirely at peace until they have done something—something more than what the exercises in this book have so far suggested. It is for those people that I have written this chapter.

As I see it, there are currently two "peace movements" going on in the United States, one of which is based on the still-prevailing mass belief system and which I'll call the antiwar movement; the other, based on the emerging belief system, I'll call the true peace movement. These two movements are, of course, vastly different in their philosophies and approaches. The antiwar movement sees mankind as hostile, dog-eat-dog, competitive. The focus is on war as the ultimate evil, and the approach is to "make" people aware of this evil in the hope of enlisting them on the side of "good"—going to war against evil. Anyone who does not believe as they do is their enemy. The enemy is not only Russia, or communism, or whatever but also anyone in the United States or elsewhere who, for example, supports nuclear power. They use fear tactics to "win" people to "their side," and they use anger as a means of empowering themselves (for they believe themselves to be basically powerless otherwise). They believe nuclear holocaust to be imminent, that time is running out, that it may have run out already. They fear that no one will survive such a scenario, as if "survival" were an acceptable goal. Basically they have little faith in humanity, believing man's nature to be self-destructive. They see peace as a dim possibility some time in the distant future.

On the other hand, the true peace movement sees the world and mankind as an interconnected, interdependent ecosystem. The focus is on peace and the inherent goodness of all life, and the approach is to hold this vision in the mind and imagination. They believe that each of us has the power to create his or her own reality and to create (and change) the mass reality. They have faith in man's good intentions and know that the planet is undergoing a paradigmatic shift; the world has learned the lessons it had to learn under the old system and is in the process of forming a new belief system—a system that no longer values mere survival as a goal but recognizes and values life as a highly dynamic, highly creative, always growing and changing process. They value peace and know how it *feels,* now.

As you can see, the antiwar movement focuses in on war, keeping it in the imagination and thereby giving it power: Hating war manifests war. The true peace movement focuses in on peace, keeping it in the imagination and thereby giving it power: Loving peace manifests peace. It seems to me there is no doubt which of the two approaches is more effective. So the first step in creating world peace is to replace the beliefs you have (which all of us have to varying degrees) that fall under the "hating war" category with ones that are in keeping with "loving peace."

As we have seen throughout this book, denying your beliefs or making part of yourself wrong for having them creates a war within yourself, which is counterproductive. Therefore, it is best to get all of these beliefs out in the open where the conscious mind can look at them. I have listed some of these in the exercise section that follows. Observe these beliefs with compassion and play with them as a child would. See what results these beliefs have in terms of feelings, actions (or lack of action), memories, your future. Realize—and this is important—that you are not your beliefs. Your beliefs are a means of expressing yourself, and you can always change your means of expression. After all, you wouldn't call your luggage you, or a painting you created you. You can always change your luggage, and you can always paint a new painting. And the same is true of your beliefs.

It is also useful to keep in mind that if love and peace were not the norm, if love and peace were not "winning out," then we would have been annihilated long ago. Remember what I said in chapter 3 about tending to notice the negatives in life because they stand out from the basically harmonious background? Well, the same is true on a worldwide basis. We need to keep the same perspective on the world as we do on ourselves as individuals: The norm is harmony.

Perhaps the most prevalent belief underlying hatred (fear) of war is that someone "out there"—the enemy—is controlling your life. There are people or forces who can do you in without your being able to do anything about it. The more amorphous that outside force is, the less power you feel you have. Thus it may seem that in your daily dealings you are in control of your own destiny, but when it comes to the decisions of government or of another country you feel helpless. If you are aware of this belief in you, it is important to notice all of the ways in which you do have power, to affirm continually the everyday evidence of your self-power. Look at the daily decisions you make that lead to the creation of one reality over another. Realize that wars exist because people buy into a belief in their powerlessness— they reflect back that belief. See how ridiculous such a belief really is as you think of what a unique human being you are and *know* absolutely that no power on earth (or elsewhere) can take away your uniqueness. You are yourself and always will be.

If you feel you must "do something" in order to support this belief in your power, then find your own way of helping others to see their beliefs and to give them support and encouragement in changing them. Point out to them the power they do have and always have had to express themselves in their own unique way. And, by extension, see also that each nation on earth is unique, with its own self-created characteristics. The idea that one nation can take over another and impose its characteristics on that other is as ridiculous as the idea that anyone can force you to see the world in exactly the way he or she does—or, for that matter, that anyone could "steal" your unique perspective. It is true that nations have been taken over militarily, but the mass consciousness that made up that nation was never vanquished. It continued to express itself in its own unique way. Over time, it may have chosen to take on some of the beliefs of its "conquerors," but it never became a carbon copy of that other nation. Rather, *both* nations changed.

Each nation is composed of unique entities, each with his or her own viewpoint, and en masse they make up a nation-entity with its viewpoint. Just as no other entity can ever have your exact view of the world, so, too, no other nation can view the world in quite the same way as a neighboring (or a far away) nation can. A good example of this is the difference between China and Russia under communism. The same ideology was proselytized in both countries, and the people took it up. Some would say they were "taken over." But look at how different the two countries still are. They are no more similar now than they were before they embraced the same ideology. In fact, I think they are even *more* different from one another now.

I want to conclude by making the point that love and hate are not opposites. Rather, hate is love with fear attached. The hatred of war that so many people feel, from this perspective can be seen as the love of peace—with fear attached. "I love peace but am afraid I can't have it.'' In hating war you create the very reality you fear. By believing in peace you create peace.

At some time you may have hated someone close to you because you feared you were separated from his or her love. Similarly, some of us now hate other nations because we feel separated from the love that unites all people. In desiring and believing in our natural intent to love, we can bridge the separation and love the other countries and their people as we can do, and have done, with our intimate others.

Exercise

1. Here is a list of some of the prevalent "hate war" beliefs. Put a check after all of those you have experienced at one time or another.

   a. I am powerless.
   b. I cannot create change.
   c. There will never be peace.
   d. The Russians are our enemies.
   e. There is a lot of evil stuff out there.
   f. Evil (hate) is more powerful than good (love).
   g. If we don't defend ourselves, we'll get taken over.
   h. I don't have a future.
   i. Nuclear power is evil.
   j. The holocaust is nigh.
   k. Man has a warlike nature.
   l. It's them against us.
   m. I can't change the world.
   n. Peace is a long way down the road.
   o. Wherever there are people there are wars.
   p. People who support nuclear power are my enemies.
   q. It's a dog-eat-dog world; every man for himself.
   r. Time is running out.

2. List all the emotions you have created from those beliefs: fear, anger, powerlessness, etc.
3. List all the emotions that come from believing in peace: love, harmony, power, beauty, grace, etc.
4. Write down the beliefs that create those emotions.
5. From now on, notice all of the peace-loving aspects about yourself. Notice yourself when peaceful and celebrate this inner harmony. Rejoice in every event that reflects a belief in peace. Create experiences for yourself that support a belief in peace, whether it be discussing peace with others, saying prayers, writing letters to the editor, or another means of expression that feels right to you.

Habit of Happiness #23

Visualize world peace!

Notes

Notes

Notes

Notes

Notes